AMNESTY

AMNESTY

THE AMERICAN PUZZLE
EDWARD F. DOLAN, JR.

FRANKLIN WATTS

NEW YORK • LONDON • 1976

THIS BOOK IS FOR ZELDA
FINE MOTHER, FINE FRIEND

Library of Congress Cataloging in Publication Data

Dolan, Edward F   1924–
   Amnesty: the American puzzle.

   Bibliography: p.
   Includes index
   SUMMARY: Discusses the issues involved in granting amnesty to Vietnam war deserters and draft evaders, including a
history of the protests against the Vietnam war and a descrip-
tion of President Ford's amnesty program and its results.
   1. Amnesty—United States—Juvenile literature. 2. Vietnamese Conflict, 1961–1975—Conscientious objectors—
Juvenile literature. 3. Vietnamese Conflict, 1961–1975—
Desertions—Juvenile literature. 4. United States—Politics
and government—1945–   —Juvenile literature. [1. Amnesty. 2. Vietnamese Conflict, 1961–1975—Conscientious
objectors. 3. Vietnamese Conflict, 1961–1975—Desertions. 4. United States—Politics and government—
1945–   ] I. Title.
DS559.8.A4D64   959.704'31   75–34358
ISBN 0–531–02845–3

ACKNOWLEDGMENTS

For their help in the preparation of this book, appreciation is due to the American Civil Liberties Union; the Project on Amnesty of the American Civil Liberties Union; the National Council of Churches; the United States Department of Justice; the United States Department of Defense; and the Selective Service System. All were most helpful in supplying needed material.

A special word of appreciation goes to William Royse of San Rafael, California, for his assistance in the research into the backgrounds of the Vietnam involvement; and to Richard B. Lyttle of Inverness, California, for his encouragement and editorial comment.

A particular debt is owed the seven draft resisters who explained their feelings of the time and those of their fellow deserters and evaders. They have asked not to be mentioned by name.

Finally, I wish to acknowledge permission to quote from the following sources:

Amnesty: The Unsettled Question of Vietnam, by Arlie Schardt, William A. Rusher, and Mark O. Hatfield; © 1973 by Sun River Press; reprinted by permission of the publishers, The Two Continents Publishing Group, New York.

The New Exiles, by Roger Neville Williams; Liveright Publishers, New York; © 1971; reprinted by permission of the publisher.

They Can't Go Home Again: The Story of America's Political Refugees, by Richard L. Killmer, Robert S. Lecky, and Debrah S. Wiley; copyright © 1971 United Church Press; reprinted with permission from Richard L. Killmer et al.

Waiting Out a War, by Lucinda Franks; G. P. Putnam's, New York; © 1974; reprinted by permission of the publisher.

"Amnesty? We're Just Beginning," an article by Arlie Schardt; *Civil Liberties,* November, 1974; reprinted by permission of *Civil Liberties,* New York.

"Amnesty," an article by Alfred B. Fitt; *The New York Times Magazine,* September 8, 1974; © 1974 by The New York Times Company; reprinted by permission.

"At a Legion Post, a Crack in the Front Against Amnesty," an article by Jon Nordheimer, *The New York Times,* October 27, 1974; © 1974 by The New York Times Company; reprinted by permission.

"Deserters in Canada Face the Agony of Decision-Making on Amnesty Issue," an article by Jon Nordheimer, *The New York Times,* September 26, 1974; © 1974 by The New York Times Company; reprinted by permission.

CONTENTS

PREFACE

Senator Edward Kennedy once called the issue of amnesty the last great national debate rising out of the Vietnam war. In the eight-year period between late 1964 and early 1973, more than a half-million men deserted from America's armed forces or evaded the draft altogether. In so doing, they separated themselves from what President Gerald R. Ford has described as the "mainstream" of American life.

These men represent a vast pool of talent for the future. The problem of returning them to that mainstream so that they may contribute to the nation's progress constitutes one of the great puzzles of our time. Should they be welcomed back because they so openly opposed a war that many later came to see as a tragic mistake? Or should they be punished because they broke United States law and turned their backs on their country in a time of need? Were they genuinely sincere in their opposition to the war or had they been interested only in "saving their own skins" while leaving others to serve and perhaps die in their place?

The puzzle is not only a difficult one. It is also one that may remain with the country for a long time to come. Views on what should be done about it often conflict sharply. President Ford attempted a solution in his "program of reconciliation" for the deserters and evaders. The program attracted no more than 20 percent of the men and has been called a failure. Various public figures and organizations have put forward their own opinions on what should—on what they feel *must*—be done. So divided are people on the issue that not one idea has won enough public and political support to be transformed into an acceptable plan.

In this book we will look at all aspects of the amnesty puzzle, beginning with a study of the word *amnesty* itself and what it has meant to nations throughout history. From there we will move to the part that amnesty has played in American history. Then we will look at how the United States became involved in the Vietnam war, at how people reacted to that involvement, at what was said for and against it, and at what was done to halt it. Finally, we will look at the puzzle itself, at the conflicting views surrounding amnesty, at the actions that have been taken for and against it, and at what the future holds for it.

In so doing, we may be better able to understand the puzzle, comment on the solutions offered, live with the solution that is finally chosen, and perhaps even contribute to the finding of that solution.

Edward F. Dolan, Jr.
June 1975

1

THE PUZZLE AND THE PAST

It was Monday, September 16, 1974. An Indian summer sun lay high and warm above Washington, D.C., as noontime approached. The new President of the United States, the first in the country's history to take the office after the resignation of the President before him, entered the Cabinet Room in the White House. He wore a striped tie and a business suit of small checks. He seated himself at the conference table that extends along the length of the room. A portrait of Abraham Lincoln graced the wall behind him.

Gerald Ford picked up a black pen and signed his name to a document that contained the phrase: ". . . pursuant to my powers under Article II, Sections 1, 2, and 3 of the Constitution, [I] do hereby proclaim a program to commence immediately to offer reconciliation to Vietnam-era draft evaders and military deserters. . . ."

With those words, President Ford attempted to close the final argument in a debate that had torn the country for more than ten years. The question of United States involvement in the Vietnam war had divided Americans everywhere—at their jobs, in their schools and churches, and in their homes, often pitting family member against family member. The war had soiled the presidencies of Lyndon B. Johnson and Richard M. Nixon. It had triggered riots in the streets and on college campuses. And it had caused more than half a million young men to flee the armed services and the military draft.

All U.S. ground troops had been withdrawn from Vietnam by former President Nixon at the end of his first term in office. Americans were eager to put Vietnam behind them, eager for a fresh start and a rebirth of national spirit. The war was pushed from the headlines by the Watergate scandal and Mr. Nixon's resignation. But one great problem still remained from the Vietnam years.

It was the problem of what to do with all those young men whose protest of the country's involvement in the war had driven them to desert the military or evade the draft. They had broken two of the strictest of U.S. laws. Some had gone into hiding and some had fled the country. What now was to become of them? They represented a great pool of talent for the future. Were they to be punished or left in hiding or out of the country? Were they to be forgiven and returned to the mainstream of American life? If so, how?

President Ford felt that he had an answer to these questions. In his proclamation, he offered them the chance to have their offenses forgotten by doing a period of public service work. He offered them, in a nutshell, a program of *conditional amnesty*.

Amnesty was a word painfully familiar to all Americans concerned with what to do about the young men. But when the debate began it was also a relatively new word, one that still felt strange to the tongue. For most of our lives, we had never had to use it. It had not been heard in the land for almost a generation—not since the close of World War II.

Now, however, it was at the forefront of American thinking. And it was a terrible puzzle. It prompted so many questions.

Would it work?

What kind of amnesty should the country grant?

What kind of amnesty would the majority of the American people accept as just?

What kind of amnesty would the young men accept?

What part had amnesty played in American history?

Did the amnesty decisions of the past open the way for granting it at the present?

What, even, did the word *amnesty* mean?

The word *amnesty* comes from the Greek *amnestia,* meaning *forgetfulness.* Amnesty is usually defined as a concept of law that permits a head of state to overlook or forget offenses committed by a person or groups of people against an authority. That authority is customarily a government.

Amnesty officially "forgets" acts that were branded as criminal at the time they were committed. They are acts, however, that rose out of political strife, and sometimes religious or racial unrest. The men, for instance, who deserted the military or evaded the draft during the Vietnam years were said to have committed criminal acts because they broke U.S. laws to which criminal penalties are attached. But the basic motive behind their offenses was political—opposition to a government that they felt to be wrong in its pursuit of the war. There were also, as we shall see later, religious and racial reasons for their actions.

The full meaning of amnesty can be seen by comparing it with a similar act—*pardon.* Both are awarded when the dropping of charges is deemed healthier for the public welfare than continued prosecution or punishment would be. Both restore to a person the legal status that he lost at the time of his offense. But each has a meaning of its own.

Pardon is customarily granted to just one person for any type of criminal offense. It is usually granted to the individual after he has been convicted. It always implies the presence of guilt or innocence; it releases a guilty person for some reason or frees an innocent man who has been unjustly imprisoned. Pardon often carries an element of forgiveness. When a guilty person is pardoned, the implication that his offense is being forgiven is unmistakable.

Amnesty, on the other hand, is almost always granted only to groups of people, to segments of the public that rose in political opposition to the government. It may be granted to members of the group who have been convicted and to those who have not been convicted. It does not imply that any or all of the people being granted amnesty are innocent or guilty. Nor does it carry any implication that they are being forgiven.

Amnesty has only one purpose—to "close the books" on the trouble. It wipes the slate clean so that the national life can proceed without further upheaval. Amnesty enables the government to pretend that the offenses never occurred in the first place.

The idea that forgiveness plays no part whatsoever in amnesty is all-important. The idea permits amnesty to accomplish three things:

First, it enables the people involved to accept amnesty without seeming to admit that they feel themselves guilty of any wrongdoing; there is, in their minds, nothing to be forgiven for. Second, it allows the government to be rid of the trouble without condoning the offenses themselves; the government is able to appear generous without showing a forgiving permissiveness that might tempt future generations to think the same offenses could be committed without punishment. Finally, if the laws or political policies that caused all the trouble in the first place have since been changed, amnesty gives the government an easy means for starting life anew; there is now nothing to forgive and so amnesty is at hand to end the whole matter. In the amnesty, the government need never say anything to admit that its former laws and policies were wrong.

Thus, amnesty has proved itself a practical governmental tool throughout history. Fair-minded nations have long disliked the idea of punishing political dissidents—citizens whose offenses are based on honest opposition to laws and policies they find odious. Such punishment can all too easily smack of oppression. And no nation likes prolonged trouble that can split its people apart. Consequently, many a country has turned to amnesty as an efficient method of restoring domestic harmony in the wake of political upheaval. Years of prosecuting the dissidents have been avoided, as have years of angry and demoralizing public debate over whether the government or its opponents were right during the period of unrest. Countless people have gone back to their daily lives; most of them were never criminals in the real sense of the word. The divisions that once split the nation have been helped, through amnesty, to heal swiftly.

Efficient tool that it is, amnesty has been used to forget a wide variety of offenses. Heading the list are treason and rebellion. Following close are the refusal to pay taxes, attempts at political overthrow, acts of disloyalty and espionage, and the two offenses that so troubled the Vietnam years—military desertion and draft evasion. When the circumstances have warranted it, amnesty has been granted for piracy and even murder. There have been instances of amnesty being declared for bigamy and polygamy.

Though it has been used to forget many offenses, amnesty is not a *right* of the people. No group of citizens in trouble with their government can be awarded amnesty on demand. In the United States, for instance, amnesty is not a constitutional guarantee, as are the freedoms of speech, worship, and the press. Rather, it is—and always has been—a *privilege* that is awarded at the discretion of a government. The government alone decides whether amnesty will or will not be declared.

Further, the government is entitled to decide the type of amnesty to be granted and the number of people to be covered by it. ·

If it wishes, the government may grant an *unconditional amnesty*. Unconditional amnesty usually forgets the offenses of all the people involved and may contain no provisions under which it is being granted. It is also called a full, general, or universal amnesty.

Or the government may opt for an amnesty that includes everyone but certain individuals. The amnesties granted by Abraham Lincoln during the Civil War were of this type. As we'll see later in the chapter, they excluded a number of people, among them Union Army officers who deserted to fight for the Confederacy.

A third choice is *conditional amnesty*. Here, the offenders are told that they will be amnestied if they meet certain provisions set by the government. They are usually asked to sign an oath of allegiance to the nation. As was the case with President Ford's program, they may be required to perform some sort of public service. At times even a full amnesty will call for the signing of an oath of allegiance.

Incidentally, some legal authorities do not look on conditional amnesty as being amnesty at all. The provisions involved, they argue, indicate that the government feels the people guilty and is using the provisions as a penance that will earn them forgiveness. Hence, conditional amnesty does not live up to the standard that guilt and forgiveness not be considered in amnesty. Further, since the provisions are less stringent than the punishment that might otherwise be imposed, the authorities feel that conditional amnesty would be better named *clemency.*

In earlier days, amnesty was always declared by reigning monarchs. With the coming of representative government, some countries placed the authority to grant amnesties with the legislative branch, while others allowed it to remain with the head of state. In the United States, the power to grant amnesties seems to rest with the President. He claims the authority from the Constitution, which states that he "shall have the power to grant Reprieves and Pardons for offenses against the United States, except in cases of impeachment."

There is a problem, however. The Constitution does not mention the word *amnesty* itself. The omission has been responsible for a number of legal debates over the years. Some authorities believe that the power of amnesty resides with the President, while others contend that it belongs to Congress.

Authorities favoring the President believe that his right to grant amnesty is implied in his right to grant pardon. In fact, they argue, his right to grant amnesty can be seen as a logical extension of the right to grant pardon. Each act has its own definition, yes, but both achieve the same end. Both restore the offender's legal status.

Those who believe that Congress has the power to grant amnesty point to the British system of law. In that system the power to grant amnesty is placed with Parliament or with the people. The U.S. Constitution was developed along lines in keeping with the British system. Thus, so the argument goes, the power to grant amnesty can be expected to rest with the Congress, which acts on behalf of the people. The debate is an interesting one and may someday be resolved.

Throughout its history, the United States has seen both the President and the Congress take a hand in the granting of amnesties. For example, at the time that President Ford announced his amnesty program, several amnesty bills were in Congress. Other examples, as we'll see in the next pages, are to be found in the years during and after the Civil War.

Amnesty probably dates back to prehistoric times, but the word itself seems to have been born in the Greece of 403 B.C. when the new leaders of Athens amnestied 3,000 supporters of the corrupt and tyrannical regime that had enslaved the city for years. Since then, in the wake of political upheaval and war, amnesties have been granted in practically every corner of the world—in such countries as England, France, Italy, Yugoslavia, Russia, India, Japan, Argentina, and Canada. In United States history, not counting the Ford program, amnesty has been granted on thirty-four occasions by thirteen Presidents.

The first U.S. amnesty was declared by George Washington in the wake of the Whiskey Insurrection of 1794. The events leading to Washington's declaration began in 1791, when Congress imposed an excise tax on alcoholic liquors, a move that outraged the farmers of Pennsylvania because it taxed their main source of income. The farmers had always found it difficult, sometimes impossible, to haul their corn crops through the often muddy backwoods to market, and so for years had distilled much of the crop into whiskey, which was far easier to transport and sell. At first, they simply refused to pay the tax, but matters soon worsened in the western area of the state. There the farmers tarred and feathered several federal tax collectors and marched on the home of General John Neville, the regional inspector for the excise. They set the place afire and it burned to the ground.

President Washington immediately ordered the insurgents back to their homes and called in 15,000 militiamen to quash the uprising. Organized resistance collapsed in the face of the advancing troops. When the dust had finally settled, eighteen farmers had been arrested. Of the lot, two were convicted for treason. The President later pardoned them.

On July 10, 1795, he took yet another step. He announced an amnesty for all who had participated in the rebellion. He proclaimed "a full, free, and entire pardon to all persons (excepting as is hereinafter excepted) of all treasons, misprisions of treason, and other indictable offenses against the United States committed within the fourth survey of Pennsylvania. . . ." Excluded were all persons "who refused or neglected to give and subscribe" an assurance of obedience to the nation's laws.

The amnesty infuriated Secretary of State Alexander Hamilton. The excise tax had been his idea, and he had pushed it through Congress with the hope that public hostility would be great, for he planned then to have the infant federal government demonstrate its power to enforce its laws by quashing the opposition. Now he was certain that Washington's leniency would undermine all that had been done. He demanded that the farmers be imprisoned, but Washington replied with a thought that is today being echoed by all who urge unconditional amnesty for the Vietnam deserters and evaders—a government must be gentle as well as firm. It must be able to forgive its people and treat them, in Washington's words, with "moderation and tenderness."

In a speech before Congress on December 8, 1795, the President said, "For though I shall always think it a sacred duty to exercise with firmness and energy the constitutional powers with which I am vested, yet it appears to me no less consistent with the public good than it is with my personal feelings to mingle in the operation of Government every degree of moderation and tenderness which the national justice, dignity, and safety may permit."

Four years later, the nation's second President, John Adams, was faced with a similar rebellion—again in Pennsylvania. This time, the trouble centered on laws that, in the opinion of some one hundred farmers, unfairly appraised their lands and buildings for taxation. When a United States marshal took several of their number into custody for refusing to pay the tax, their friends attacked him and set them free. In May 1800, after tempers had cooled, Adams amnestied the troublemakers. In wording similar to Washington's, he proclaimed "a full, free, and absolute pardon" for everyone "concerned in the said insurrection."

The nineteenth century witnessed the greatest numbers of amnesties in our history. They began with the Adams declaration of 1800 and ended in 1898 with the final amnesty act of the Civil War. Amnesties were awarded to civilians, to soldiers who had deserted in wartime, and to soldiers who had deserted in times of peace.

The first of the amnesties for peacetime desertions was proclaimed by Thomas Jefferson in 1807. Because of such factors as poor pay, primitive living conditions, and hazardous duty out on the frontiers, the Army was recording an increasing number of runaways, and Jefferson agreed to amnesty them if they would return to duty within a four-month period. Five years later, needing all the men he could muster on the eve of the War of 1812, James Madison issued a similar declaration. He did not, however, specify any exceptions or conditions, but it is thought that the returnees were made to complete their terms of military service. Finally, in 1830, Andrew Jackson declared a general amnesty for peacetime deserters after Congress had repealed a law imposing the death penalty for them. He stipulated that those in prison be released and sent back to duty. Those still at large or under the sentence of death were to be discharged and never permitted to serve again.

The amnesties for wartime desertion began with President Madison. During the course of the War of 1812, he issued two amnesties for deserters—and then added to the list one of the most unusual amnesties in the country's history. He granted amnesty to the pirates who had operated for years in and around New Orleans, men whose smuggling activities and attacks on merchant shipping had made them a terror all along the southern coast. The reason for their amnesty? They had joined General Andrew Jackson in rounding out the 7,000-man army that had successfully defended New Orleans against the final British attack in the war. Outnumbered and outgunned, the Jackson force left close to 2,000 British dead, while losing only thirteen men.

The Civil War resulted in thirty years of amnesty actions. The first three of these actions were initiated by Abraham Lincoln, who hoped to bring Southerners back to the Union by demonstrating his desire to treat them leniently. In 1862 he declared an amnesty for all Confederate political prisoners held in military custody. The welcome back to the Union demanded only the promise to give no further "aid or comfort to the enemy in hostility to the United States."

Lincoln's next proclamation, issued on March 10, 1863, was aimed primarily at those Union soldiers who had fled to fight for the South. The President understood that most of them had been raised in the South or had relatives there. He promised them amnesty if they returned to their regiments by the following April 1. Those who responded were returned to duty and received no punishment other than the loss of pay for the time of their absence.

Additionally, the President pardoned a number of deserters on an individual basis. They were mostly men who had deserted and had not gone over to the Southern side. He usually sent them back to their units with the instructions that they were to serve as long as their commanding officers deemed necessary.

Then, at year's end, Lincoln appealed to the widest audience possible. On December 8—the sixty-eighth anniversary of Washington's "moderation and tenderness" speech—he offered amnesty to all Confederate sympathizers, soldiers and civilians alike, who wanted to "resume their allegiance to the United States." For them, he proclaimed that "a full pardon is hereby granted . . . with restoration of all rights and property, except as to slaves and in property cases where the rights of third parties shall have intervened."

He set just one provision. Each returnee had to sign an oath of allegiance to the country:

"I,_____, do solemnly swear, in presence of Almighty God, that I will henceforth faithfully support, protect, and defend the Constitution and the Union of the States thereunder; and that I will in like manner abide by and faithfully support all acts of Congress passed during the existing rebellion with reference to slaves, so long and so far as not yet repealed, modified, or held void by Congress or by decision of the Supreme Court; and that I will in like manner abide by and faithfully support all proclamations of the President during the existing rebellion having reference to slaves, so long and so far as not modified or declared void by decision of the Supreme Court. So help me God."

Though Lincoln tried to reach the widest audience possible, he did exclude a number of people from the amnesty offer. Among those excluded were: Confederate diplomats and foreign agents; Confederate officers above the rank of colonel; officers and enlisted men who had mistreated captured Union soldiers; officers who had resigned the Union Army to join the Confederate Army; members of Congress who had left their seats to side with the Confederacy; and anyone who had attempted to destroy U.S. commerce at sea or on the Great Lakes.

The amnesties granted by Lincoln were all part of his plan to welcome the South back to the Union once the war was over. He wanted to see the country reunited without any revenge taken on the people of the Confederacy. The policy that he planned for the post-war years was one of gentleness, such gentleness that it was dubbed "rose water sweet" by those in Congress who felt the South should be punished.

Lincoln's whole attitude toward the South was expressed in a statement that he once made during a meeting of his Cabinet. The Cabinet members were discussing the possible punishment of Confederate leaders once peace was restored. Lincoln listened for a time and then said: "I hope that there will be no persecutions, no bloody work after the war is over. No one need expect me to take part in hanging or killing those men, even the worst of them. . . ."

Lincoln himself was not given the chance to put his postwar policy into effect. On the night of April 14, 1865, just five days after the war closed with the surrender at Appomatox Courthouse, an assassin's bullet ended his life. His practice of granting amnesties, however, was continued by his successor, Andrew Johnson.

No fewer than five amnesties were granted by Johnson. The first was declared on May 29, 1865, to all who would swear allegiance to the Constitution and promise to support the new laws regarding slavery. He excluded the same people whom Lincoln had excluded in December 1864. But he added one more exception to the list. Excluded were all Southern landowners who had voluntarily participated in the rebellion and whose taxable property exceeded $20,000. Born of a poor family, Johnson had long envied the wealthy plantation class, and this was his way of trying to prevent them from regaining political power in the South.

Approximately 140,000 people took advantage of the amnesty in the next months. Further, Johnson stated that those on the excepted list could make special applications to him for pardon. Several thousand Southerners, wanting to avoid punishment for the rebellion and eager to vote for the legislatures being formed in their states, applied for pardon. Johnson soon earned the reputation of approving almost every application that came his way. He was not only a poor man but a vain one. The wealthy Southerners whom he so despised now won pardon by fanning his ego and treating him as a social equal.

The number of pardons angered and frightened many members of Congress. They saw that the very people most responsible for secession were now being returned to power. Many were running the reconstructed states. Some were seeking congressional seats. If elected, they could do much to hamper or prevent the passage of legislation necessary to the restoration of the Union.

What could be done about the situation? The question brought to the forefront the old question of who has the authority to grant amnesties—the President or Congress. Congress now put the question to the test by making a change in a major bill that had been enacted in the early war years—the Confiscation Act.

Passed in 1862, the act provided severe penalties, including imprisonment and the confiscation of property, for those convicted of supporting the Confederacy. It contained, however, what was called a "clement clause," a section that authorized the President to amnesty any convicted Southerners as he saw fit. (Believing in the presidential power to grant amnesties, Lincoln had refused to recognize this assertion of congressional authority when he had issued his proclamations, and Congress had not argued the point with him.) Now, to combat Johnson, the angry legislators repealed the clement clause and claimed all amnesty powers for themselves.

Johnson, also a believer of presidential authority in the field, ignored the claim. He issued three new proclamations—on December 18, 1866; September 7, 1867; and July 4, 1868. Each reduced the number of people on the excluded list. These proclamations drove many in Congress to seek his impeachment, a compaign that missed seeing him removed from the White House by the slim margin of just one vote. He then declared a universal amnesty on Christmas Day, 1868, striking the last people from the excluded list. This was the final presidential amnesty of the Civil War.

But the drama was not yet ended. In 1866, Congress had failed in an attempt to have the Fourteenth Amendment ratified. Now, in 1868, a new attempt succeeded. Contained in the amendment was a section meant to keep many Southerners out of positions of influence. It held that any federal or state officer who had once sworn allegiance to the Constitution and then had sided with the Confederacy could not again hold office. It further stated, however, that the official could be taken out from under this cloud by a two-thirds vote of the Congress.

As far as approximately 160,000 people were concerned, this section nullified the amnesties that had been granted by Johnson. Congress now began the process of clearing them on an individual basis, a process that continued for thirty years. Two bills—one in 1871, the other in 1872—helped matters by granting amnesty to all Confederates except three hundred to five hundred of their leaders. Finally, in 1898, a universal amnesty for those leaders was announced. It was considered as little more than a gesture to comfort their families and close the books on the Civil War. By that time most of the men who had stood at the Confederate helm were dead.

In that very same year, a situation arose that brought the country to its next instance of amnesty: 1898 marked the end of the Spanish-American War, with the United States winning from Spain the islands of Cuba and Guam and the entire Philippine Island chain. Further trouble, however, erupted in the Philippines. Philippine troops under Emilio Aguinaldo had helped the American Army oust the Spanish. Aguinaldo said that his people wanted their independence and had no more intention of submitting to American rule that they had to Spanish. Some historians believe that the United States had promised Philippine independence in trade for Aguinaldo's help and then had infuriated him by reneging on the promise. His men took up arms and fought a guerrilla action against American troops for the next five years.

In 1902, with peace restored, President Theodore Roosevelt amnestied all who had participated in the Philippine Insurrection—or, as it was called in the islands themselves, the Philippine War of Independence. (The islands were later granted their independence, at the close of World War II.)

The amnesties awarded in the years following the Philippine uprising were all on a small scale. Woodrow Wilson offered no amnesty after World War I, but Calvin Coolidge in 1924 amnestied all men who had deserted the Army after the Armistice of November 1918. In 1933, Franklin D. Roosevelt followed suit by pardoning all World War I draft evaders who had been sentenced and had served terms in prison. The actions of both Presidents were taken to restore to the men their citizenship, which they had lost because of a 1912 decision by the Supreme Court. The Court had ruled that crimes against the federal government resulted in the loss of citizenship.

Against the threat of world domination by the Axis powers, few Americans opposed U.S. participation in World War II. But even then, President Harry S. Truman had to face the fact that an estimated 15,000 to 16,000 men had evaded the draft or otherwise violated the Selective Service Act. Rather than handling them as a group, he elected to have their cases individually investigated and judged. He appointed a three-man Amnesty Board to the task in December 1946.

The board looked at 15,805 cases throughout 1947. In the end, it recommended that 1,523 deserved pardon and the restoration of their civil rights. Mr. Truman proclaimed an amnesty for them on December 23, 1947.

Five years later, he declared another amnesty, this time restoring the civil rights of all men who had deserted—or who had been court-martialed and dishonorably discharged for desertion— between the end of World War II and the Korean war. No amnesty of any sort was proclaimed in the wake of the Korean conflict.

The word was not to be heard again until late in the 1960s. By that time, the United States was deep in a war that was being called the most brutal in the nation's history.

2

THE VIETNAM WAR

Vietnam is a small, narrow country that, with its coastline curving down alongside the South China Sea, lies just off the southeastern edge of China. A land of 127,300 square miles that divides itself between rugged mountains and fertile deltas, it claims a history as turbulent as any to be found in the world, a history whose turbulence reached its zenith in the twentieth century.

That history began in 111 B.C. when the Chinese advanced into the northern regions of the country and established the kingdom of Namviet. Challenged from time to time by the northern people, the kingdom held sway until it was overthrown in the tenth century A.D. and was replaced by the Li Dynasty, a family of native rulers. The Li emperors in the next years moved steadily southward until the nation, all along its slender length, lay in their hands.

The move, however, was not made without difficulty. First, the dynasty fought off Mongol armies that swept in from China with an eye to making the land their own. Next, the people of the south long and stubbornly resisted the Li before at last being subjugated. And next, beginning in the fifteenth century, the Vietnamese endured the Dutch, Portuguese, and British, who first came to trade and then stayed to seek economic gain and political influence. Finally, the

French came. Using Vietnam's emperor as a puppet, the French won control of the entire land during the 1800s and rounded out the century by bringing neighboring Laos and Cambodia under their control. The threesome, then known as French Indochina, enriched France with their resources until the outbreak of World War II.

On the eve of World War II, the people of Vietnam were a diverse lot. Their number included not only the Vietnamese themselves but also great numbers of Chinese, Cambodians, and Thais. They ranged across a social scale from rice farmers and primitive hill tribesmen to city merchants and businessmen, and along a religious spectrum from Buddhism and Confucianism to Roman Catholicism. But, diverse though they were, they seemed of a single mind on one point. They wanted to be free of French domination. They wanted theirs to be an independent nation.

Throughout the decade prior to the war, they persistently agitated for that independence. Their efforts, however, were quite as diverse as the population itself. The people were not banded together in a single nationalist organization, but were splintered into a number of freedom groups and movements, with the memberships determined along religious, political, and socioeconomic lines. Some groups were manned by Buddhists, others by Catholics, others by communists, others by businessmen, and still others by farmers. From this splintered collection, though, one group finally managed to gain prominence.

It was the *Viet Nam Doc Lap Dong Minh*—the Vietnam League for Independence. Better known simply as the Viet Minh, it took shape in the northern regions when a number of noncommunist and communist groups banded together for greater strength. Despite its noncommunist elements, however, its leadership was mainly communist. At its head was a veteran disciple of Marxism, Ho Chi Minh.

Very soon after the outbreak of war, France fell to Germany, with the loss of much prestige in Vietnam. Ho, seeing that loss as a new opportunity for furthering his independence aims, increased the Viet Minh's harassment of the French planters, businessmen, and troops in their midst. Then, when Japanese troops arrived in Vietnam, he was quick to resist their presence. This resistance caught American eyes and marked the beginning of United States involvement in Vietnam.

The United States spent the first months after Pearl Harbor mounting a counterattack against Japan. When America's attack was launched, American troops were dispatched up the curve of the Pacific from Guadalcanal to the Marshall and Solomon islands and on to Formosa just below the Japanese homeland. The counter-attack also sent U.S. troops to the Chinese mainland, where they joined Generalissimo Chiang Kai-shek in fighting Japan's soldiers there. Once in China, the U.S. saw the strategic vatue of neighboring Vietnam. It was easy to recognize that whichever side held the upper hand there could easily outflank the other in China.

Though U.S. feelings were not yet as hostile as they were to become in the 1950s, the Americans in China had no liking for the communist-led Viet Minh. But they could not overlook what Ho and his fighters were doing to hamper Japan's aggression in Vietnam. And so, to make certain that Japan did not become too powerful a flanking force, the U.S. offered to give Ho money and arms for his fight in exchange for intelligence reports on Japan's activities. Ho accepted, and then proved of service in yet another area. His guer-rilla fighters often rescued Allied fliers shot down over Japanese-controlled territory. Upon returning them to safety, the guerrillas were given a reward, usually $1,000 in gold. At times, they also received additional military supplies.

As soon as the Pacific war ended, leaving Japan defeated and the French colonial authority in ruins, Ho moved to seize power, declaring Vietnam independent and establishing a government at the northern city of Hanoi. Ho's authority, however, embraced only the northern one-third of Vietnam, for the south was in the hands of nationalist groups formed principally along religious lines. Fortu-nately for Ho, they were at odds with each other. The Viet Minh leader sent his agents southward to bring the southern groups under his leadership. They succeeded in drawing various of the southern organizations together under what Ho called the Committee of the South.

Another name must now be mentioned—that of young Viet-namese Emperor Bao Dai. With the rest of his countrymen, he had long sought independence for the nation, but he had done so in the war by cooperating with Japan. He envisioned a freedom for Vietnam, but one that would be under Japan's "supervision." The plan, of course, collapsed with Japan's defeat. The emperor, realizing that Ho was perhaps the most influential man in the country, asked him to form a provisional government. Its purpose was to bind the country together and supervise its business until a formal nation could be established.

When the provisional government was formed on August 29, 1945, Ho declared himself its president, for he felt that the emperor's cooperation with Japan had rendered Bao unfit for rule. On September 2, he announced a Vietnamese Declaration of Independence. He began it with the very words that Thomas Jefferson had penned for the U.S. Declaration: ". . . . all men are created equal. They are endowed by their Creator with certain unalienable rights, and among them are life, liberty, and the pursuit of happiness."

At the time, and in the years thereafter, many Americans looked on the document as a strange one to be coming from a communist leader. They saw it as an effort on Ho's part to win U.S. support for his provisional government should the French try to regain control in Vietnam. And perhaps it was, at least in part. But there is also reason to think that Ho looked on the United States with genuine affection. Had not the United States itself been born, as Vietnam was being born, in the turmoil of throwing off the yoke of foreign domination? And hadn't the United States and Ho cooperated in fighting Japan?

American support, however, was not forthcoming. It went, instead, to France, which was given back its Indochina colonial empire when the Allied powers met at Yalta in 1945 to determine the postwar fate of the Axis. The United States, traditionally and spiritually opposed to colonial expansion, disliked seeing Vietnam returned to France, but it believed that, were not France in power there, the entire country would soon be dominated by Ho and his communist followers. In giving its blessing to the French reconquest, the United States took the first of many steps to stall the advance of communism wherever it was to be found. That commitment became a cornerstone of American foreign policy in the following years.

French efforts to regain control of Vietnam—backed by $2.6 billion in American aid between 1950 and 1954—resulted in seven years of bloody warfare and intricate political maneuvering. Politically, the French reinstated Bao Dai as the chief of state in the southern Vietnam area, but with limited powers under their authority. Militarily, Ho and the Viet Minh fought an unending guerrilla action, attacking or sabotaging French installations and plantations and then fading into the jungles and forests. In 1954 the Viet Minh finally emerged as a conventional field army and attacked the vast French fortification at Dien Bien Phu, a broad valley close to the Cambodian border. For two months, 40,000 Viet Minh troops laid siege to the fortification before at last attacking it directly on May 7. They swarmed over the battered defenses and took some 16,000 French troops prisoner. With the collapse of Dien Bien Phu, French influence in Vietnam, which had begun to crumble in World War II, was at an end.

What now was to become of Vietnam, suddenly free of French control, but with its southern area led by Bao Dai and its northern regions in Viet Minh hands? That question went before an international conference at Geneva, Switzerland. The conference—cochaired by Great Britain and Russia, and attended by representatives from the United States and France, together with representatives from North and South Vietnam—hammered out what looked to be a simple solution.

The country was to be temporarily divided into two states—North and South Vietnam—at a line roughly approximating the 17th Parallel. Ho would remain in power north of the line, and Bao Dai south of the line. Each state was to withdraw its forces back to its own side of the line. The people in the north and south were to be given three hundred days to determine on which side of the line they preferred to live, and then to move accordingly. In two years' time, an election was to be held to unify the entire country, with the people voting into power the government they desired.

Simple though the solution looked, it posed a problem for the United States. Ho Chi Minh was undisputedly a remarkable leader and so popular with the people both north and south of the 17th Parallel that they had long ago nicknamed him "Uncle Ho." The United States feared that, at the time of the unification election, they would vote him into power. The new nation would become a communist state. Worse, the United States feared that, once all of Vietnam was in Ho's hands, the other countries of Southeast Asia would be vulnerable to communist domination. In the words of the U.S. statemen of the day, they would fall "like a set of dominoes."

And so the United States threw its support behind South Vietnam. There, the government was now headed by Premier Ngo Dinh Diem, who had been placed in charge by Emperor Bao. Diem was an ardent anticommunist and a long-time advocate of Vietnamese independence. The aim of U.S. support was to help him develop a prosperous state that would attract more voters than Ho's government in the planned unification election.

American support of the Diem government was at first principally economic. In the seven-year period between 1955 and 1962, the U.S. supplied South Vietnam with $2 billion in aid, of which $1.4 billion went to agricultural reforms intended to increase crop yields and place in peasant hands large tracts of land once held by the French. Additionally, the U.S. assigned military advisors—685 of them in the beginning—to assist in the training of the South Vietnamese Army.

Those seven years saw a disenchantment with Diem spread through the United States. He proved himself anything but a democratic leader. He stood accused of executing his political enemies by the hundreds and imprisoning them by the thousands. There were reports that he and his closest supporters were cornering many of the American supplies and profiting from them—and reports that high-paying political posts in the South Vietnamese capital, Saigon, were being filled by his relatives and relatives' friends. Americans came to understand that U.S. money was being spent to support a corrupt regime. Still the aid continued. The commitment remained to build a prosperous society that would defeat Ho in the unification election. American leaders found the idea of a communist Vietnam more frightening than that of a corrupt government in the south.

So bad did matters become in the south that a group of influential Vietnamese politicians, religious leaders, and high-ranking army officers demanded Diem's resignation. He countered the ultimatum by calling for a general election and placing himself on the ballot as a candidate for president. On the surface, it seemed a democratic move: let the people themselves decide whether he was to remain at the head of the government or be ousted. Behind the scenes, so the reports of the day held, he "rigged" the election by coercing the voters and suppressing the opposition.

On taking office, he renamed the country the Republic of South Vietnam. Then he announced that there would be no future unification election. He gave as his reason the opinion that no such thing as a free and representative vote of the people could be obtained in North Vietnam.

Ho Chi Minh was outraged by the announcement. He had liberated Vietnam from the French and had counted on his popularity to win him control of the entire nation. Now the chance to do so had been snatched from him. There was only one thing that he could do. He must fight.

He began that struggle with an army of underground fighters—the *Viet Cong San*, meaning the "Vietnamese Communists," and best known simply as the Viet Cong. The Viet Cong had long operated under his direction in South Vietnam, their intention being to disrupt the activities and progress of the Diem government. But now they began to bring as much southern territory as possible under their wing, doing so by assassinating village leaders, attacking military installations, and sabotaging plantations and industrial facilities. That the South Vietnamese Army was unable to stop them is seen in the fact that they eventually dominated much of South Vietnam's coastline and most of its rice-rich Mekong Delta. By 1964, some 74 percent of South Vietnam was said to be in Viet Cong hands. Saigon, the capital city, was itself ringed by VC guerrilla forces, with some as close to the city limits as twenty miles.

Americans watched the situation with growing frustration. South Vietnam was failing on two counts. Not only was it headed by a corrupt government (Diem was assassinated in 1963, but the new leaders were considered no better than he) but its modern and American-equipped army was showing itself incapable of defeating a band of tattered underground fighters.

Still, the U.S. commitment to stall the advance of communism in Southeast Asia remained. American military and economic aid mounted steadily. By the end of 1961, thirty-three helicopters, along with four hundred pilots and technicians, had been sent to the little republic, and the original force of 685 advisors had risen to 2,000. In February 1962 *The New York Times* reported that 5,000 Americans were on Vietnamese duty; the figure had jumped to 11,000 by year's end. Ten months later, in November 1963, the total stood at 16,500. Then 1964 dawned. For Americans, it proved to be the most critical year in Vietnam to date.

It was the year that recorded two alleged North Vietnamese attacks on the U.S. destroyer *Maddox*, once while the ship was patrolling alone in the Golf of Tonkin off the North Vietnamese coast, and once while in the company of a fellow destroyer, the U.S.S. *C. Turner Joy*. On both occasions, the attackers were PT boats, which were reported to have fired torpedoes at the Americans. The fire was returned, and three of the PT boats were sunk in the first of the engagements. On neither occasion were the destroyers struck or otherwise damaged.

The Ho government justified the attacks by charging that the American ships had been participating in a South Vietnamese naval action along the North Vietnamese coast. The American government insisted that the destroyers had been on routine patrol and could have played no part in the coastal action for they had been a prudent twenty-five to thirty miles out to sea at the time. Washington immediately ordered retaliatory air strikes against North Vietnam from the carriers *Constellation* and *Ticonderoga*. An angry President Lyndon B. Johnson went before Congress and asked for the authority to intensify U.S. military action in Vietnam. He worded his request in a resolution that became known as the Gulf of Tonkin Resolution.

The resolution stated that "the Congress approves and supports the determination of the President, as Commander in Chief, to take all necessary measures to repel any armed attack against the forces of the United States and to prevent further aggression." The resolution passed the House of Representatives unanimously and cleared the Senate by an 88–2 vote, with senators Ernest Gruening of Alaska and Wayne Morse of Oregon dissenting. Congressional anger over the fact that American ships had been attacked was not alone in accounting for the overwhelming vote given the resolution. The legislators were also worried by government statistics showing that a North Vietnamese Army division—numbering from 14,000 to 25,000 men—had joined the Viet Cong in South Vietnam. To many a concerned senator and representative, the little country seemed in desperate need of additional help if it was to keep from falling into communist hands.

Later, the Gulf of Tonkin Resolution became the center of an angry controversy, with critics of the U.S. involvement in Vietnam charging that Mr. Johnson had lied to the Congress and the public when pressing for its passage. Regardless of whether the President lied or told the truth, the resolution opened the door on one of the costliest and most brutal wars in history.

It was a war that, in time, graduated from a struggle with the guerrilla Viet Cong to conventional field battles with the North Vietnamese Army. It was punctuated throughout with massive air strikes against North Vietnam, against the Viet Cong in South Vietnam, against communist forces in neighboring Laos, and finally against another neighbor, Cambodia. The United States committed as much as $78 million dollars a day to the war, spending $28.8 billion in 1969 alone.

But the cost in money was nothing compared to the price in human life and pain. Two and a half million American soldiers, airmen, and sailors went to Vietnam. Of their number, 45,937 were killed in action, while 10,303 died of noncombat causes. Approximately 30,000 sustained wounds and injuries.

Altogether, including civilian deaths, the struggle claimed 1,763,000 lives. Statistics showed that 184,089 troops were lost by South Vietnam, and 929,692 by North Vietnam and its Viet Cong. Australia, New Zealand, South Korea, and Thailand—all of whom joined the U.S. effort—reported losses totaling 5,225. Civilian deaths in both the north and the south numbered over 600,000.

The land itself was devastated and its fertility jeopardized for generations to come. The weapons of modern war—bombs, napalm, artillery shells, and chemical agents—deprived more than 10 million South Vietnamese of their homes, their farms, and their villages. The homeless, who were assembled in makeshift camps or who wandered from place to place in search of shelter, finally totaled more than two-thirds of the tiny country's population.

Opposition to this holocaust and to the American role in it was quick to take shape. It was an opposition that eventually drove more than a half-million men to turn their backs on the military and the draft. It was an opposition that began with the nation's youth—students and workers who were in such revolt against all aspects of American life that they were known as the "protest generation."

3

WHEN THOUSANDS SPOKE

Youthful unrest has always played a part in history, but the young people of the 1960s were a particularly involved group. They criticized established views and institutions and defiantly turned away from the way things had been before.

University students rebelled against a traditional and, as they called it, mechanistic approach to education. Militants stood at the head of the civil rights movement and were turning it away from a nonviolent campaign for equality. Countless young people joined the "hippie" counter-culture with its disdain for luxury and long-established values. Young men and women of political bent charged that the poor were being exploited by industry and government, that the nation was in the hands of an industrial-military complex, and that American carelessness and greed were destroying the country's beauty and befouling its air and water.

This spectacle of unrest left older people—not to mention the many students not involved in it—speechless and bewildered. The opinions as to its cause were many. Some people held that the young were the "spoiled brats" of permissive parents and had not been taught the disciplines necessary for success in a competitive society; now, unable to cope with that society, they were trying to break it as if it were an unwanted toy. Others believed that modern young Americans, living in a prosperous society that did not require them to work from an early age, had the leisure to study current problems and then take action against the institutions apparently responsible for them. Still others theorized that, for some unknown reason, the generation of the 1960s had managed to break out of that "shell of self" that had always separated people from each other. The shell had long made people selfish and competitive. Today's young were reaching out to each other, trying to become a part of each other, and they could not help but lash out at those traditions and institutions that seemed to stand in their way.

All these opinions were merely guesses. Only one thing could be said for certain. Regardless of their many angers, the young people were united on one issue: all hated the part being played by the United States in the Vietnam war.

American participation in the fighting could not help but arouse their disgust. To pacifists, war defied the credo of every civilized religion: thou shalt not kill. For those demanding a better life for the minorities and the poor, the military draft was known to be swelling army ranks with blacks, Chicanos, and men from the nation's less affluent groups while bypassing the sons of the privileged and middle class. For those of political bent, the nation seemed to be pursuing the war for the benefit of the U.S. military-industrial complex and doing so at the sacrifice of programs needed for human enrichment. And for all who were dedicated to a freer and more equal society, the war was interrupting the lives of thousands of young people, forcing them into a little-understood—and, they suspected, useless—conflict not of their making.

The dislike of the war was first clearly seen during the months following the Gulf of Tonkin Resolution, months in which the American troop build-up in Vietnam began to take frightening shape. The first outcries, however, came from just a few pacifist groups. The Student Peace Union, the War Resisters League, the Central Committee for Conscientious Objectors, and the Quakers—all spoke out against a danger that to them seemed obvious. The May Second Movement, composed of young people dedicated to the political and philosophical ideas of Maoist China, staged a march against the war and signed a pledge not to serve in Vietnam. But these embryonic protests went unheeded by the general public. The average American—including the average American college student—looked on the groups as being too radical for their views to be trusted.

In 1965, however, as Air Force bombings began to level Vietnam and as the U.S. troop build-up passed the 100,000 mark, the resistance spread from just a handful of pacifist groups to vast numbers of students. Suddenly united were the diverse elements of the "protest generation." Joining them were countless young people who had never before given politics more than a passing thought. Together, they moved out along two fronts. They protested the war itself and then lashed out at the military draft that collected the men for the fighting.

The first widespread opposition to the war itself was voiced in what were quickly called "teach-ins." They were meetings held on college campuses to debate the pros and cons of the involvement in Vietnam. Attended by students and teachers alike, the discussions, though sometimes punctuated by angry demands for violent antiwar measures, were quiet, objective exercises in the democratic process at work. The views aired were many and varied, for the participants represented a broad range of American outlook.

Some students supported the government and believed that it was honoring a commitment to South Vietnam. They agreed with the political leaders who held that, if Vietnam were allowed to fall into Ho's grasp, all the countries of Southeast Asia would, in keeping with the domino theory, quickly succumb to communism.

On the opposite side of the fence were those who insisted we had become entangled in a struggle with distant forces that posed no real threat to our future welfare. Others claimed that the United States could not possibly win the war. The North Vietnamese, they argued, had ousted France with its superior arms; now the Viet Cong guerrilla fighters, as familiar with the defenses of the countryside as they were, would assuredly defeat the Americans. Others contended that the United States, with its superior weaponry, was shaming itself before the world by destroying a peasant nation. Still others condemned all American military actions, demanding that the government stop trying to stamp out communism in every small and unde-veloped country. They charged that America's "adventures" abroad were as much intended to protect its foreign investments and its global prestige as to combat the "Red Menace." They were tired of the nation's self-imposed role as the "world's policeman," and they wanted Washington to turn its attentions from making war to develop-ing programs to meet the needs of the American people.

The teach-ins began at the University of Michigan in March 1965 and continued throughout that year and into the next. The largest and most publicized of the teach-ins took place on May 22, 1965, at the University of California's Berkeley campus. It attracted an estimated 12,000 people, both students and nonstudents, and lasted for some thirty-six hours.

The teach-ins failed to halt or slow the war effort. They had no effect on the increasing call for military manpower; monthly draft calls jumped to 35,000 (previously, they had been 6,000) by the spring of 1965 and reached the 45,000 mark by December. Nor did the teach-ins impress the government. The bombings continued. Several lead-ing political figures accused the participants of being traitors. Presi-dent Johnson approved a Justice Department probe of the antiwar movement to see if there was "communist involvement" in it.

But the discussion sessions did achieve one major goal. Pre-viously, opposition to the war had been limited to small groups. Now, thanks to months of quiet debate, the antiwar movement was solidify-ing and word of it was spreading to thousands of students who had been hitherto uncommitted to or unaware of its aims.

At the same time the teach-ins were being launched, the first of the antiwar demonstrations began, led by young people who pre-ferred, as they put it, "to vote with our feet" rather than their voices. In April 1965 some 25,000 students and their supporters triggered the demonstration trend by rallying in Washington, D.C., to publicize their sentiments. Thereafter, for a period of five years, the demonstration was to prove one of the most popular of antiwar weapons.

Within weeks of that April rally, a number of peace and politi-cal groups, chief among them the Students for a Democratic Society (SDS), joined forces to plan a series of demonstrations to be known as the "International Days of Protest." They managed to field 80,000 marchers in several cities for the first day of protest, which was held in October 1965. But close to two years later, in April of 1967, with misgivings about the war now spreading rapidly to the older generations, a massive day of protest was organized. It drew countless people of all ages to marches held in large cities and small towns; participants ranged in number from mere handfuls in rural midwestern communities to crowds estimated at between 100,000 and 250,000 in New York City. The "March on the Pentagon," a demonstration that jammed the streets of the nation's capital with more than 100,000 people, all chanting antiwar slogans, also occurred in 1967. Further marches were held in 1968 and 1969, with the latter year recording another demonstration of more than 100,000 people in Washington, D.C.

For the first two years of their history, though marred periodically by violence, the demonstrations were peaceful in nature. But 1968 marked a change. For two reasons, violence now became the trend.

First, there was a growing frustration within the antiwar movement over the government's persistent—stubborn, it seemed to many—refusal to heed the protestors. Monthly draft calls were continuing to rise. Some young men who refused to be inducted into the Army were being sent to prison. President Johnson was still sticking to the words he had addressed to a television audience back in 1965: "We will not be defeated. . . . We will not withdraw, either openly or under the cloak of a meaningless agreement."

Second, the movement was being more and more influenced by the militants in its midst. They contended that the government would never respond to reason but only to a massive show of force, one that would cripple the United States capacity to make war.

And so, beginning in 1968, violence increasingly dominated antiwar tactics. That year alone saw two turbulent outbreaks. In April students invaded the administrative buildings at Columbia University in New York City and held them against police while demanding that the Institute for Defense Analysis, a government-financed unit that used the school's facilities to research new techniques of warfare, be kicked off campus. (The students also insisted that the university cancel plans to build a gymnasium on a nearby piece of land used as a park by a black neighborhood.) Then, in August, thousands of young demonstrators clashed with police at the Democratic National Convention in Chicago, treating the American television public to the spectacle of widespread rioting.

In later years, the Marine Midland Bank, the Chase Manhattan Bank, and the Manhattan Federal Building—all located in New York City—were bombed for their connections with the war effort. There was antiwar rioting in Chicago in 1969. The violence was climaxed with the deaths of five students within the next year. In 1970 four students were felled by bullets during protest demonstrations at Ohio's Kent State University. Shortly thereafter, a graduate student died when the math and physics building at the University of Wisconsin was bombed.

Though the teach-ins of 1965 heard a number of conflicting views, most of the participants agreed on one point. From the most conservative to the most radical, they spoke out bitterly against the U.S. Selective Service System—the draft.

In particular they branded the draft unfair. They pointed as proof to its various deferments for students and the technically skilled. They claimed that the deferments protected the affluent, those with the money or the prior education to attend college or acquire a skill needed by the economy. Left as "cannon fodder" for the draft were the sons of the working class, the poor, and the minorities. The young people found this unfairness so apparent that they early dubbed Vietnam "the poor man's war."

They also found the draft unfair in yet another way. They argued that it snatched up a young man, put him in uniform, and sent him off to war without letting him have any say in the matter. He could not refuse because he found the war useless, dangerous to America's future, or morally objectionable. Regardless of his personal aspirations, he was made to live a part of his life as the government wanted him to live it. He had no voice in whether he would live or die.

From being a matter of discussion at the teach-ins, the draft protest became a definite movement. Early in 1965 a number of University of California men demonstrated their refusal to serve in the military by burning their draft cards. A little later in the year, nine pacifists attempted to disrupt the work of New York's Whitehall Induction Center by blocking its entrance. Still later, five young men stood before a crowd of 1,500 in New York City and publicly set their draft cards afire. In 1966, sixty-six Princeton University seniors announced they would not fight in Vietnam. Two hundred Cornell University students soon followed suit.

The government reacted angrily to the first signs of draft resistance. Congress imposed a $10,000 fine and a prison sentence of up to five years for draft card burning. Then, after thirty-five University of Michigan students staged a sit-in protest at a nearby draft board, the director of the Selective Service System, General Lewis B. Hershey, recommended that they all be drafted. Within a month, nine of their number had been declared delinquent or reclassified 1-A (the top category for induction) by their local draft boards.

The protest, which had begun on a small scale, grew quickly, thanks mainly to the example set by the first men who refused to fight. By 1967 resistance to the draft was massive. It was of both a private and public nature. On the private side, thousands of young men were said to have secretly burned their draft cards and resolved never to serve. Thousands more had refused the summons to induction and now, aided by friends, were in hiding. Some had refused to hide and had been sent to prison or were awaiting trial.

On the public side, there was a rising cry to kill the draft law and its hated deferments. Twenty thousand demonstrators marched through New York City in May, their placards—worded "Hell No, We Won't Go"—looking stark and defiant in the springtime air. In October 1,000 protestors gathered at the Oakland Induction Center to disrupt the swearing-in of new recruits; 119 demonstators were arrested. The year ended with a December "Stop the Draft Week," with draft cards being returned to the Justice Department from men in more than thirty cities. Students across the country called for the removal of the military recruiting stations and tables that had been for so long a feature of the campus scene. Some 3,200 delegates attended an antidraft conference and demanded that the Reserve Officers Training Corps (ROTC) also be banned from colleges everywhere.

As did the general antiwar movement—and for the same reasons—the draft resistance turned to violence in 1968. Now small groups of militants took to setting fire to a number of campus ROTC buildings. The Whitehall Induction Center, the Selective Service office in Berkeley, and the draft board offices in Madison, Wisconsin, and Lancaster, Pennsylvania—all were bombed. The draft board office at Milwaukee, Wisconsin, was burned, and even the Selective Service headquarters in Washington, D.C., was entered and a small fire set. In Catonsville, Maryland, nine Catholic resisters broke into the draft board office and set six hundred files and records ablaze. Two priests who are brothers—the reverends Daniel and Philip Berrigan—accepted the blame for leading the raid, saying that they and their companions were protesting a system that defied peace and humanity by sending young Americans to die in a senseless war.

The violence that came to play such a part in both the war and draft protests alarmed many people. Among them were a number of resistance leaders who felt that every riot, every fire, and every bombing damaged their cause by showing that the demonstrators were not really visionaries interested in ending the war and building a new world, but spoiled children intent only on tearing down the traditions and institutions that their elders held dear. How, one California leader asked, could anyone believe in their expressed dedication to peace when so many of them contaminated their movement with the thing that was the very opposite of peace? A quick answer came from the militant among the demonstrators: the public and the government paid no attention to soft words. Violent acts were needed to get their attention and convince them that the anti-Vietnam campaign was a serious one.

Despite the widespread criticism of the violence, the anti-Vietnam campaign had made remarkable strides by the close of the 1960s. For example, the government in 1969 responded to the demands that the draft law be changed. The deferment system was dropped and replaced by a lottery in which a man's call-up date for service was determined by his birthday. Many young people felt the lottery was not much of an improvement, for it left a man's military fate to be determined by chance alone. But, at least, it did get rid of the discriminatory deferments.

Better yet, there was increasing public and official talk of dropping the draft altogether. Predictions were heard that the draft would soon be replaced by an all-volunteer army. The predictions came true in 1973.

Best of all, the war and draft protests had helped alert the older generations to the horrors of the Vietnam involvement. By the 1970s, the views concerning Vietnam held by most Americans were changing dramatically. Surveys taken in the early sixties had shown a majority to favor the war, seeing it as the government's effort to honor a commitment to South Vietnam and halt a communist takeover there. But a 1972 Gallup Poll revealed that 73 percent of the people interviewed were disenchanted with the involvement and wanted our troops brought home. They set just one proviso: they wanted the troops withdrawn only if the U.S. servicemen captured by the North Vietnamese during the fighting were set free.

The anti-Vietnam campaign was greatly responsible for this change of heart. Special credit went to such older protestors as Senator Eugene McCarthy, Nobel Prize scientist Linus Pauling, and baby specialist Dr. Benjamin Spock. In speaking out against the war, they had caught the attention of people whom the young demonstrators by themselves could not have reached. But the antiwar and draft movements could not claim full credit for turning a majority of the population against the Vietnam involvement. Other factors had also played a significant part.

To begin with, people were tired of the war. It had dragged on for years and seemed no closer to a solution now than it had back in 1965 when Secretary of Defense Robert McNamara had announced the certainty of a quick American victory and a return of our men by Christmas. There had been no quick victory then, and now, in the 1970s, there was still no victory. Some people felt that the United States had not won—and would never win—because political limitations had been imposed on its troops; for instance, America had never sent ground units into North Vietnam itself, in part because of a fear of then having to fight neighboring China. Others thought that the North Vietnamese and the Viet Cong had simply battled a mighty nation to a standstill.

Further, countless Americans had lost faith in their government, a situation that the press immediately dubbed "the credibility gap."

They felt there was ample reason for the loss. As one businessman put it, "Our leaders kept telling us that we were winning, but the truth seemed to be that we weren't. I felt I was being lied to." Another echoed the sentiment of many when he said, "We were supposed to be saving a country from communism. Instead, we were destroying it with our bombs and chemical poisons."

Further, those forces in government that most favored the war appeared to be taking dangerously irregular steps to quiet the opposition. The Army stood accused of spying on the political activities of civilians, activities that were constitutionally protected. Led by President Nixon, factions in government were attacking the media for expressing an antiwar stand and seemed to be trying to throttle the freedom of the press. The Attorney General was saying that he had the right, without the permission of the courts, to wiretap or spy on anyone whom he suspected to be a national security risk.

To Americans in great numbers, the nation seemed to have lost its democratic sense and to be fast becoming a "police state."

And they felt that this democratic sense had been lost out of fear. For years the government had feared the danger of international communism, and feared that one day it would topple the United States. That fear had spread to the people and had prompted them to agree with the official stand that the fall of Vietnam and then of all Southeast Asia like a set of dominoes would be a disaster for America. But now times were changing. Communism no longer struck all Americans as a personal threat. The fear of it was passing. With it was going the support of the war.

Worsening the whole situation were the charges that former President Johnson had lied to Congress when pressing for the Gulf of Tonkin Resolution. He had said that the North Vietnamese PT boats had fired on the American destroyers; there was now evidence that the PT boats had fired no shots at all. He had pointed to government reports showing that an entire North Vietnamese division had joined the Viet Cong in the South. Records of the time had since been found in Washington. They revealed that the "division" numbered not thousands of men but only four hundred or so.

Clearly, so the charges held, the inept South Vietnamese Army was being defeated by a relatively few men, and Mr. Johnson had lied so that he would seem justified in sending a massive force to South Vietnam in place of the few military advisors already there. He had needed to manufacture a "great danger," and the Gulf of Tonkin incident had enabled him to do so. Without that "great danger," the world would have criticized the United States for assigning countless men to the fighting. America would have appeared a bullying aggressor rather than a noble defender.

The President's motives were further attacked. Some of his critics said that he had committed the giant force out of blind pride; as he himself once said, he had no intention of being the first President to "preside over an American defeat." Others claimed that economic aims were behind the presidential move that turned the conflict into a major war. All those U.S. industries that thrived on war were profiting mightily from Vietnam.

Besides being angry with their own leaders, many Americans had lost faith in the South Vietnamese government. President Diem had been assassinated by political enemies back in 1963 and the government had changed hands several times since. It was purportedly a democratic government, but the indications were that it was not. There were reports that its leaders were siphoning off American money and military supplies for their own pocketbooks, reports that the press was controlled by the government, and reports that the government had imprisoned, without trial, as many as 100,000 South Vietnamese who dared to speak out against it. These reports indicated yet another loss in the U.S. democratic sense. Traditionally, America was opposed to dictatorial governments. But here it was supporting a government that, though anticommunist, appeared to be as corrupt and as harsh as the worst of dictatorships.

The accusations of corruption in Vietnam were not limited to the government. They were extended to the American troops there. There were rumors of our soldiers profiting from the "black market" sale of stolen U.S. supplies. There were statistics on the use of drugs by an alarming percentage of our troops. And there was the realization, horrifying people all across the United States, that our troops were responsible for atrocities committed against the Vietnamese people.

The most publicized instance of brutality was the "My Lai massacre," in which American infantrymen fired into groups of women and children during a raid on a village said to house Viet Cong fighters. The Army court-martialed the officer on the scene,

Lieutenant William Calley, but at the same time insisted that the soldiers had acted out of an understandable fear. They were fighting, the Army said, a vicious adversary not in an identifiable uniform and so had to regard every civilian as a potential enemy. It was an argument that didn't sit well, especially when so many of the dead were women and children. On the heels of My Lai came reports that it was not the first incident of its kind.

Many Americans could understand the war profiteering. They didn't like it, but they knew it was historically an evil connected with any war. But drug usage and the killing of women and children— these were matters that shook practically every American to the core. Had this useless war that promised no victory so frustrated and dehumanized our men overseas that they had turned to drugs for solace and to animal brutality as a release for their passions? Or were the atrocities and the drugs—the latter in widespread use here as well as abroad—symptoms of something that had sickened in the American character over the complex and confusing years since World War II? No one really knew the answer. All that could be said was that drugs and brutality were present in Vietnam. Our men must be removed. A fresh start must be made in the life of the United States.

And so a variety of factors—ranging all the way from exhaustion with the war to a growing disgust of U.S. conduct in Vietnam and at home—finally soured a majority of Americans on the war. The early 1970s were marked by a rising cry to end the involvement. It was a cry that eventually hastened the end of the draft and the beginning of President Nixon's efforts to sever the Vietnam ties. Attempts were made to strengthen the South Vietnamese Army so that it could fight on alone. Negotiations for the return of U.S. prisoners of war were completed. The prisoners and the troops began the return home. The last U.S. combat units departed Vietnam on March 23, 1973.

But, for thousands of American men from all walks of life, the end came too late. Years ago they had made their decision to have nothing to do with Vietnam. To stay beyond the reach of the military, they were hiding at home or living abroad.

4

EVADERS AND DESERTERS

Between early 1965 and mid-1972, more than a half-million American men refused to fight in Vietnam. The first to refuse were those who resisted the draft. They were soon followed by men in uniform who fled from U.S. posts all across the world.

The very first of the young men who rebelled against the draft in 1965 did not go into hiding in this country or flee to a foreign nation. They took their stand—as did the five resisters who burned their draft cards before a crowd of 1,500 in New York City—out in the open for all to see. Then they remained out in the open, waiting for the arrest, trial, and imprisonment that seemed sure to come.

They felt that they could not do otherwise. They said that their defiance of the military was an act of conscience and courage, but that it would not be interpreted as such if they fled or went into hiding. The public could then properly brand them as cowards who, behind a façade of righteousness, were really interested only in saving their own skins. No one would ever be convinced of their courage, their sincerity, and their devotion to their cause if they failed to "stand up and be counted." They had to face the consequences of their action.

Further, as one early draft resister explained, "We wanted to get the reasons behind our antiwar stand over to the public. We couldn't do this if we were in hiding or out of the country. But if we were arrested and had to stand trial—well, that would put us right in the limelight. We could speak out and the people would hear. Maybe they would get to understand how we felt and get to hate the whole Vietnam thing. Then maybe there would be enough of them to pressure the government into ending the whole thing."

The leaders of the antiwar campaign encouraged the first resisters in their determination to stand and face the authorities. The leaders understood that the general public regarded the earliest peace advocates as unstable and untrustworthy radicals. But that attitude, they felt, would surely change when the country saw thousands of apparently solid and sensible young men willingly put their futures on the line and accept punishment for their beliefs. Such a spectacle would certainly trigger a nationwide appreciation for and support of the anti-Vietnam campaign.

Additionally, the leaders wanted the courage and the sacrifice of the first resisters to serve as an inspiration for the countless men still trying to reach a decision about the draft. If enough men could be inspired to opt against induction, then eventually there would not be enough soldiers to conduct the war. The result would be to cripple our efforts in Vietnam and quickly end the war.

This desire to jam the gears of the military was behind much of the early talk about the unfairness of the draft deferments. Many antiwar leaders wanted to see the deferments dropped not just to give the working and poor classes a break but to goad the nation's several million college students to fury. They reasoned that, so long as countless young men remained safe in college, there would never be a truly major outcry against the draft. But, vulnerable to induction once their deferments were gone, the students would be outraged, and there would be a massive resistance that would eventually collapse the military. It was a mistaken view. When the deferments were discarded and replaced by the lottery system in 1969, there was no crippling resistance.

For several reasons, the resolve "to stand their ground" did not last long among the resisters. First, the general public of the mid-decade showed as little sympathy for their actions as it did for the entire anti-Vietnam campaign; the nationwide disenchantment with the war still lay in the far distance. Second, while the draft card burnings and the refusals to be inducted did inspire a growing number of men to balk at service, the military was not in the least throttled; there were ample draftees and volunteers for the fighting. Finally, there seems to have been in the resisters of 1965 a sense of martyrdom, a willingness to go to jail for their cause, that was not to be found in those who followed.

The attitude of the later resisters was recently voiced by one Californian as he looked back on his own feelings in those days. "I didn't want to go to jail, period. I hated the war, but I was no sacrificial lamb. I valued my freedom too much. And jail wasn't doing any good, anyway. It wasn't changing anybody's mind about anything or ending the war. It was just locking a guy up and stalling his life. There had to be another way."

The other ways?

"If we didn't want to end up in prison, we were left with four choices—all of them bad. We could be drafted. We could apply for conscientious objector status. We could try to stay out by tricking our draft board. Or we could take off."

Why were the choices, in the Californian's words, "all bad"?

Again reflecting the attitudes of the resisters, he answered, "The first one is obvious. In all conscience, you just couldn't take even the smallest part in a war you knew was immoral. It would have been a cop-out to allow yourself to be drafted just so you wouldn't have to stand the heat from your family and friends. And an even bigger cop-out to go in and then worm yourself into a nice safe berth and let somebody else get killed.

"And suppose you weren't one of the lucky ones. Suppose you ended up in combat. It would have been murder to kill someone and immoral to let your own body be violated, because you were in an unjust and senseless war, not defending your country, not doing a thing but jumping through a hoop that the military wanted you to jump through."

On conscientious objector status:

"There was one thing wrong with CO status. Most draft-age men simply couldn't qualify for it."

At the beginning of the resistance, the basis for granting conscientious objector status was as it had been for years. As written, the CO law required an applicant to prove that his conscience would not let him participate in a war by reason of his "religious training and belief." He could not object to fighting because he held views that were "essentially political, social, or philosophical" or views that constituted "a merely personal code." If he managed to qualify, he could choose between serving in the Army as a noncombatant or performing civilian work that would "contribute to the maintenance of the national health, safety, or interest."

Most draft-age men immediately recognized that they would never qualify. Their opposition to Vietnam was grounded mainly in political, social, and private moral objections. Further, most could not claim that they had been trained in a religion that saw all war as unjust; that sort of belief was limited to a handful of religious organizations. Finally, the requirement for CO status always brought up a question to which most could not truthfully answer with a "yes": Do you, in conscience, object to all wars?

So the CO status was an impossibility for most, and it remained so even after a decision by the Supreme Court in the mid-sixties. In what was known as the "Seeger Case," the Court broadened somewhat the "religious training and belief" clause to include outlooks that were not necessarily traditional or totally religious. Though the way was opened to objection on the grounds of personal conscience, CO status was still hard to come by. It was granted by local draft boards and they had the right to question all applicants closely. Many of the young men, regardless of the sincerity of their convictions, could not satisfactorily explain their objections to the war. Some did not have the educational background in philosophy for adequate explanation. Some did not have the vocabulary. And the ideas of some were too cloudy.

As for "tricking the draft board":

"That," the Californian said quickly, "was dishonest, a way of keeping out without ever standing up and saying your piece. A lot of guys stayed out for the whole war that way. They'd go 4-F [a classification that excused men from service because of health problems] by getting a sympathetic doctor to write up some ailment for them—something that would be hard for the Army to disprove, like a bad back or a trick knee from playing football. Or they'd move from town to town just to keep their records moving around so there would be less chance of some local board tapping them on the shoulder and saying, okay, man, it's your turn. Or they would literally shop around until they found a board that would accept their excuses for staying out."

Most resisters, the Californian pointed out, felt no pangs of conscience about tricking the draft board on a temporary basis. "We felt it quite right to avoid service for as long as we could. The government people were trying to get us killed for no reason at all, and so we had the right to stall them whenever we could. But to stay out for the whole time by fooling with the draft? No way. That was an ultimate dishonesty that we couldn't buy. We were honest in our opposition to the war. We had to be just as honest with the draft board in the long run. Sooner or later, we had to speak out, had to draw the line."

Finally, on "taking off":

"To a lot of people, that must have looked like the easy way out. But it wasn't. Whether you went into hiding in this country or moved to a new country, you knew you were in trouble. You had to break away from your family, your friends, your girl. You had to put aside your plans for the future. You had to put up with a lot of anger and heartbreak back home.

"If you hid out in this country," the Californian went on, "you were always scared stiff that you were going to get caught. If you went to some other country, you couldn't just settle down and make yourself comfortable. You were afraid because you had to get used to new ways—even a new language—and figure out how to make a living. You had to build a whole new life. You had to realize that you might never be going home again."

He shook his head. "No, sir. They weren't good choices. But, if we were to follow our consciences and not play the Vietnam game, we finally had to settle on one. For myself, I ran."

In running, he and his fellow resisters became lawbreakers and the objects of much public scorn. They became draft evaders.

Especially despised were those evaders who went to live in

foreign countries. Many Americans branded them as cowards who had escaped punishment and were living openly and safely while others were sent to Vietnam to die in their place.

The evaders living abroad, however, regarded themselves as anything but cowards. They agreed that foreign residence put them beyond the reach of U.S. law and enabled them to live openly. But there was more to their move than just that. Some saw the U.S. as a dictatorship and military machine that promised them no future; it drove them to go elsewhere to start life anew. Others said that they were going into exile. In so doing, they were making an open, honest political statement. They were telling the world of the depths of their convictions about Vietnam; so deep were their convictions that they were willing to abandon their families, their futures, and their country for them.

There was nothing cowardly, the evaders insisted, in the search for a new and free life or in the making of an honestly felt political statement.

Men in uniform who objected to the war soon followed the evaders. They were helped to their decision by peace advocates who opened coffee shops near military bases and then used them as places for meeting with soldiers to explain the antiwar stand. Soon, inside camps here and abroad, servicemen were forming committees to criticize the Vietnam involvement and to publish antiwar newspapers and pamphlets for distribution among their fellows. These first outcries triggered a flow of desertions that quickly swelled to a flood.

It must be noted immediately that not all desertions stemmed directly from antiwar or antiservice sentiment. Many men fled to escape prosecution for acts having nothing to do with the peace stand—acts that ranged from insubordination to disorderly conduct, theft, and rape. Further, the military defines desertion as "being absent from duty for more than thirty days without official leave." For one reason or another, a number of men assuredly ran off for just a short time and then, accidentally or deliberately, overstayed the time limit. Had they returned sooner, they would have faced the far less serious charge of being AWOL—absent without official leave.

But there seems little doubt that a major share of the desertions could be traced to what the men were seeing and not liking about the war and the military.

Said one deserter, "The bombings and the stories about all the civilians being killed. That's what really got to me. I decided I just couldn't be a part of it any more."

Another said that he had disagreed with the war while he was in college. From all that he had read, he was pretty certain that the U.S. involvement was a mistake, but he wasn't absolutely sure. "Then I lost my student deferment and got drafted. As soon as I got to Vietnam, I learned that all I had been reading was true. The war was brutalizing us, making animals of us. I served out my tour and was shipped home. Then I did what I should have done before I ever let myself be drafted. I took off."

Still another said: "I admired the evaders. They were making a statement against the war. I had wanted to do the same thing when I got my draft notice. But I hadn't had the guts for it. I worried about what my family and friends would think. I had thought that I'd be ruining my life. But, finally, I just couldn't keep quiet any longer. I had to make *my* statement."

A number of blacks, keenly aware of the civil rights struggle, deserted because they felt unable to fight any longer for a country that exploited their race in the draft. Angrily, they recalled Martin Luther King's statement that nearly 22 percent of the troops in Vietnam were black, while blacks constituted only 10 percent of the U.S. population.

One black claimed that angry white reaction to the civil rights movement drove him to desert. He had never been aware of discrimination as a boy. But, on returning home from Vietnam, he became so conscious of what he called "hate stares" that he concluded the United States had gone "ugly." He ran off to Canada. His story strikes especially hard when it is known that he was not a drafted soldier but a volunteer.

A great number of men, black and white alike, deserted when they found they could not abide service life. They called it a life full of "restrictions" and "inhumanities."

For instance, one soldier said that he could no longer stand being hit in the stomach by the sergeant who was displeased with the poor way he stood at attention and the even poorer way in which he cleaned his rifle.

Another claimed that he fled because of the beatings he received while serving a sentence for drug usage.

One thought his superiors "ridiculous." He said they kept talking about "kill, kill, kill." He decided that he could no longer tolerate it.

One said that he could not abide the regimentation of army life. "It was like being cooped up all the time. All the time, there were people telling you what to do, where to go, how to stand, how to think. There was no room to be yourself."

And many, in attempting to describe their feelings about the war and the service, could give no single, rational reason for their desertion. They had seen too much of war, too much of what the bombings and the fighting and the napalm had done. They seemed reduced to the inarticulate. Perhaps one of them said it all when he remembered, "I think I was going out of my head. I just had to get out."

And get out they did. Between the mid-1960s and the close of 1972, no fewer than 495,689 American servicemen fled from bases in this country, in Europe, and in Vietnam. Desertions reached their peak in 1971. The Army alone that year reported the loss of 79,000 men; the loss equaled six full divisions. In all, the years of desertion cost the military the equivalent of 5 percent of Army and Marine Corps strength.

One point, however, must be remembered. Approximately 90 percent of the deserters returned to their bases voluntarily or were apprehended by military authorities. Left were between 32,000 and 50,000 runaways. Some went into hiding here in the United States. Others concealed themselves with native friends in Vietnam. And still others joined those many draft evaders who were taking sanctuary in foreign countries.

Where did they go and how did they make out?

5

THE EXODUS

The sight of young men fleeing abroad was a spectacle strange to American eyes. In years past, countless people from over the world had come to the United States to find a new life. Now, between late 1965 and early 1973, the process seemed reversed.

Some two hundred men chose France, while another two hundred or so opted for Great Britain; settling there, in the main, were evaders arriving from the U.S. and draft-age students afraid to go home once their studies in European universities were completed. Between six hundred and eight hundred men went to Sweden, with at least twenty-five of their number being deserters from Vietnam who made their way there via Japan and the Soviet Union, helped along by student groups and sympathizers in those countries. Denmark, Ireland, and Italy harbored an undetermined—but known to be small—number of men. By far the greatest contingent of men went to Canada. It was estimated that at least 30,000 men went to Canada, but some officials there felt that the total may have run as high as 60,000.

For the most part, the Americans met little difficulty when entering exile. Great Britain, for instance, admitted the evaders as visitors and awarded them work and student permits. The deserters,

however, were a different matter. Desertion was regarded as a serious offense, one committed by men who—regardless of whether
they were draftees or volunteers—had taken an oath to fight for their
country. Britain felt that it could not harbor such individuals and so
closed its doors to them. As for the evaders, it held them to be private
citizens on whom the military had no claim. They were free to travel
wherever they chose. Unless Britain itself could find their behavior or
backgrounds undesirable, it saw no reason to refuse them admission
on a temporary basis.

France initially allowed both evaders and deserters to enter.
The latter came mainly from U.S. bases in Europe. In time, feeling
much as Britain did and not wanting to rupture its relations with the
U.S. government, France also shunned the deserters.

Both evaders and deserters were admitted to Sweden on an
individual basis, with the country granting work and residence permits to most newcomers, while turning away just a few. Turned away
were those who, for such reasons as personal conduct or past criminal activity, were deemed unfit for entry. In general, Sweden looked
on its acceptance of the Americans as a humanitarian gesture, one in
keeping with its long-standing commitment to peace and its neutrality
in world clashes.

Canada, likewise, accepted both evaders and deserters. Its
immigration laws took no notice of the military status of anyone wishing to visit or settle in the country. Further, Canada is a nation traditionally opposed to military conscription. It also viewed America's
involvement in Vietnam as a tragic mistake, a danger to world peace.

Much was done in some of the countries to make the newcomers feel welcome. In Canada and Sweden, many of the Americans were invited to stay in private homes during the first difficult
months of adjustment. The Swedish government, in keeping with its
policy for immigrants, paid the Americans' rent and gave them $18 a
week for food and clothing until they found jobs. In Canada, at least
twenty aid centers for the exiles sprang up across the country.
Manned by Canadians and the exiles themselves, they assisted new
arrivals in getting their bearings, finding jobs and lodgings, and meeting new friends. Many Americans, liking what they saw and wanting
to protect themselves against any possibility of future deportation,

applied for citizenship in Canada and Sweden. Of the more than 30,000 draft-age Americans in Canada, some 16,000 applied for landed immigrant status, the first step along the road to full citizenship.

It would be a mistake, though, to think that every man settled easily into his new country. Certain factions within each nation objected to the arrival of the Americans. Some people disliked the newcomers simply because they were strangers. Others complained that the exiles would overcrowd the job market. Others prophesied that they would swell the welfare rolls. And still others, as did a few Canadians, labeled them "misfits" and "cowards" and demanded that the government deport them. The Canadian press reacted angrily to the demand, with the *Calgary Herald* saying that "it would be dangerous for the nation to set up barriers to entry in the clouded areas of personal conscience and conviction. It has always been the boast of free countries that they can be a refuge for noncriminal foreign exiles."

By far the greatest obstacles to settling down were the personal burdens that each exile carried. Remember the words of the Californian. "You were afraid. . . . You had to put up with a lot of anger and heartbreak back home. . . . You had to try to build a whole new life."

His words are echoed by the several writers of the day who reported on the problems encountered by the exiles. In his book *The New Exiles,* Roger Neville Williams wrote of the fear in the first men to go to Canada:

"They were understandably afraid; *paranoid* is the common word. Would they be arrested and shipped home? Would they be met with hostility if it were learned that they had refused to go into the United States Army? There was no way to find out in those days. The first war resisters must be credited with a special courage, since it took courage for a young American, with no one to follow, to take his life into his own hands and strike out to find a place where he could live."

Mr. Williams also spoke of the scornful anger that reached out from home to the exiles. The public, ignoring their claim that they were making a brave political statement, branded them as cowards and traitors who should be executed or at least imprisoned. Though it had been expected by all the exiles, the outrage still wounded some deeply and filled them with guilt and self-doubt. But what really hurt was the fact that the anger was not limited to just the public in general. It was shared by many of their friends and by many in the peace movement itself, all of whom should have appreciated what they were doing.

Mr. Williams, himself a resister who went into exile, explained: "Going to Canada was a 'cop-out' from the struggle. Occasionally, antiwar organizers, with an easily forgotten medical deferment, told those bound for Canada that they were cowards. Even more significant was that men in Canada would get letters from home, perhaps from a girl, which said: 'We know so-and-so who beat the draft by faking a trick knee. He says anyone with a little brains can get out of the draft; you don't have to go to Canada. He thinks you're a fool to be up there.' . . . If that wasn't psychologically devastating, nothing was, and it happened in one way or another to nearly every war resister in Canada."

Equally—perhaps even more—devastating were the reactions of many an exile's family. A few young deserters and evaders were encouraged by their antiwar parents, with some routinely receiving economic help and words of kindness from home. But most had to live with the knowledge that they had shocked, bewildered, hurt, and, in some instances, infuriated their people. They had dealt wounds—to their loved ones and themselves—that might never heal.

Richard L. Killman, Robert S. Lecky, and Debrah S. Wiley wrote the book *They Can't Go Home Again* at the height of the exodus to Canada and Sweden. It was a study of the flight, and in it they reported on the anguish of many parents:

"Many parents of the young men who emigrated to Canada and elsewhere are hostile to their sons' act, viewing military service as an honorable obligation. Often fathers have fought in previous wars and are proud of their service record. Even more important, most of these parents live in an environment which shares and reinforces this understanding of military service and obligation. Local young men seem to enlist for service and submit to orders to go to Vietnam without resistance.

"Parents tend to view their resisting son as a disgrace. To hide this disgrace they will not tell their friends or relatives, nor will many religious families even tell their clergyman. Instead, to hide their shame and prevent ostracism, they will deliberately isolate themselves. One pastor in Maryland has ministered to three such sets of parents after the sons informed him they were in Canada; the parents had been too ashamed to confide in him their sorrow and anxiety."

The book contained a letter sent by one mother to her exile son. The authors said that it illustrated the "extreme depth of fear and anxiety" to which some parents were driven. Here are portions of that letter:

"What can I say to a son who has become a deserter and traitor to his country, family, and friends? You know that is what you are. You really had us proud of you and now you ask to be referred to as a man. You must be kidding. A man is not a sniveling coward who has to run away from any form of authority or discipline just because it is temporarily inconvenient. You must really be a feather in the cap of your Godless communist friends. . . .

"You claim to love us and miss us. I don't think you are capable of real love for anyone or you wouldn't have done this. You say you hope you don't hurt us too much. Well let me tell you something, it would have been more merciful if you had killed us all before you left. You didn't have to watch your brother cry and cry, your grandma and Aunt D_____ get sick. . . . As for me, I am on the verge of being committed to Danville. Nice thoughts, aren't they? No, you didn't hurt us—you killed us. . . .

"You will have to make up your mind. Search your heart and if you decide to come back, all you have to do is write or call. This is the only time you will hear from us. Your decision will affect your brothers' lives also. They will never be able to get any kind of job where security is involved, because there will always be doubt.

"You have taught us a lesson though. Don't ever be too happy or proud and brag about your children because you get kicked right in the teeth. You have hurt your father so deeply, because he thought you two were really close together after all these years. I hope you can walk with your head in the air."

The letter, as said before, was an extreme one. But even those letters less biting—those that spoke of not understanding a son's motivations or that voiced a tearful concern for his welfare and his future—could not help but upset the recipient. For his principles, he had damaged the lives of the people dearest to him. Further, every exile knew that he had left his family vulnerable to problems with the U.S. authorities.

As the authors of *They Can't Go Home Again* pointed out: "Parents sometimes bear a particular burden at home with respect to legal authorities. It has been reported that the F.B.I. has visited parents of deserters and resisters. They have been known to harass them, sometimes entering the parents' home without a search warrant or telling the parents of their legal rights. A black mother in Detroit with speech and hearing problems was visited by the F.B.I. four times. In none of the visits did the F.B.I. show her a search warrant. In a harsh manner, including obscenities, they asked her the whereabouts of her son, a deserter. They visited her neighbors and harassed one who had severe emotional problems. . . ."

On top of all else, all but the most insensitive of the young men had to endure a period of terrible psychological upheaval as they adjusted to a new life. They were in strange countries and, if they had gone to Sweden or France, up against strange languages and unfamiliar customs. Not only did they feel guilt for what they had done to their families, but now, with their flight an accomplished fact, they had to endure anguished moments of wondering whether they had done the right thing. And, if they were among the very first arrivals, they had to carry with them a sense of awful aloneness. They were, as practically every writer of the period has put it, disoriented, in a daze, wondering what to do and where to go.

Reporter Lucinda Franks, in her book *Waiting Out a War,* wrote eloquently of this disorientation when she described the early experiences of John Picciano, one of the first young American deserters in Sweden. He went to live with Olof and Else-Marie Andersson outside Stockholm. Miss Franks wrote:

"His father's letter had made him sad and homesick; the Anderssons, with their bustling, close-knit style of life, caused him to be even more homesick. The first weeks in Sweden had been a time of inner revelry. He had basked in his freedom, felt light-footed, delighted in the fact that he could live openly. . . .

"But now the reality of his situation was beginning to hit him hard. He had done something which was probably irreversible. Sometimes it seemed fantastic to him, as though he had had a long restless dream and suddenly awakened, in the middle of a strange country with no ties, roots, friends, prospects. His father had asked him to reverse the process. But that was impossible, unless he wanted to rot in some stockade. . . ."

Understanding his welter of feelings, "the Anderssons went out of their way to make John one of the family, to build up his confidence, to help ease his feelings of disorientation. They brushed up on their English. Over and over, they tried to reassure him that what he had done was valid, that in his place they would have done the same thing. He would wander from room to room, aimlessly, not hearing what people said to him. . . .

"John talked a lot about his childhood in Lodi, comparing it with the way the Anderssons lived. He became a child with them, and for a time, sensing his needs, they treated him the same way they treated their own children. He would bubble over, needing to talk to someone every moment of the day. He would follow Else-Marie around from the kitchen to the garden; he would be there when she made the beds; he followed her to the store and once even into the bathroom until it dawned on him that she wanted to take a shower and he left with great embarrassment. . . .

"The Anderssons knew that John's persistent garrulousness was necessary for the healing of his mind, knew that his incessant rattling on about unimportant as well as important matters was a way of releasing the anguish inside him. When they agreed to harbor a young refugee from a country whose youth was beginning to be torn apart by its military adventures, they knew he would bring with him fresh wounds. They realized that they were providing a thin thread for him to hang onto and so they were patient and gentle. . . ."

And so it went until John Picciano was settled in Sweden, accustomed to his new life, and active in helping his fellow exiles.

John Picciano, actually, was among the lucky ones in that he did manage to establish a new life for himself. Such was the emotional upset of many exiles that they never did settle down in their adopted countries. Many wandered aimlessly from place to place and from odd job to odd job. Some lived on the charity of friends and fellow exiles. Some seemed to be "marking time," doing nothing with their lives until the war was over and they could go home again. Many suffered a persistent homesickness; not a few Americans in Canada sneaked back over the border from time to time to visit friends and family, attend the Woodstock Music Festival, or participate in peace demonstrations. One such trip ended in tragedy when a young American was shot while trying to escape back into Canada. Earlier, he had pulled out a gun and wounded the American border guard who detected him as he was crossing into the United States.

Most of the exiles, however, settled into comfortable and fruitful ways of life after their initial sense of disorientation had passed. Many contributed their energies to such organizations as Amex and the American Deserters Committee, which were formed by the Americans to deal with the problems of the exiles and to keep tabs on political and social problems back home. Most found employment. One exile in Canada became an orchestra conductor. Another took up farming in western Canada. Several went into journalism, teaching, and medicine.

In Sweden, a survey made in 1969 demonstrated just how well the exiles there were blending into the nation's life. A total of 247 Americans were interviewed. Of the number, 104 were working, 103 were attending Swedish language classes, sixteen were enrolled at the University of Stockholm, nine were attending adult high schools, seven were in folk high schools (preparatory schools for college), and twenty were involved in vocational or other job studies. The study showed that only twenty-two of the exiles had gotten into trouble with the law, principally for drug offenses. Ninety percent of the Americans had adjusted successfully to Swedish life.

Settled though they were, the exiles everywhere began looking homeward with keen interest in the late 1960s. For it was then that the talk of amnesty began in earnest. The United States attitude toward the war had changed and was bringing the Vietnam involvement to an end. Now talk of what could be done about the exiles was starting.

What exactly was being said?

6

THE AMNESTY DEBATE

When the talk of amnesty began, Americans everywhere found themselves divided into three basic groups. There were those who believed that a full, or unconditional, amnesty should be granted. Others felt that the deserters and evaders deserved no amnesty at all. Still others felt that conditional amnesty was the wise and just choice.

Arguments for and against amnesty were voiced all across the land. Among those most often heard were the following:

Unconditional Amnesty

The major argument for unconditional amnesty was grounded in the belief that the war had been immoral and the system for drafting men unfair. Consequently, the men who had refused to participate had behaved honorably, according to the dictates of their conscience. They had refused to kill in a senseless war and had done much to awaken the American public to the dangers of the Vietnam involvement. Theirs had been a major contribution to the nation's welfare and character. They had acted correctly and so should not be punished.

Around this basic belief were built the other arguments in support of unconditional amnesty:

Illegal War

Many people held that the war, as well as being immoral, was illegal. The Constitution gives the Congress—and the Congress *only*—the right to declare war. Yet the administrations of two Presidents had pursued and widened a conflict of such proportions that it could be described as nothing other than a full-scale war. They had used the Gulf of Tonkin Resolution as a justification for what they were doing, yes. But the sheer size of the conflict, demanding so much sacrifice and threatening so many lives, had required that a formal declaration of war be announced. Congress had made no such declaration. Consequently, the war had no legal justification. The men who had refused to participate could not now be punished, for they had been resisting an illegal action.

American Tradition

Much of the argument in favor of amnesty—not only unconditional but also conditional—was voiced in the name of national traditions that had taken shape over the years. The argument was built around several points.

First, it recalled the thirty-four instances of amnesty in U.S. history. These instances, so the argument went, had long ago set a legal precedent for granting amnesty in the 1970s. Would it not be unfair to refuse amnesty now after it had been granted to the Pennsylvanians in the Whiskey Insurrection and to countless of the people who, in the greatest split the nation has ever experienced, turned their backs on the Union in the Civil War? Surely the governments of the day found their actions just as shocking as today's government found those of the Vietnam deserters and evaders— and, in the case of the Civil War, even more disquieting. What had been given to one must certainly now be given to the other.

Second, there was George Washington's "moderation and tenderness" speech in the wake of the Whiskey Insurrection. Surely it had set a spiritual precedent for the country. Hadn't it established the tradition that had been carried on by such Presidents as Lincoln and Andrew Johnson?

Finally, the argument in behalf of tradition held that the United States has always been a nation of dissenters, that, in fact, it was born in revolution. America has repeatedly welcomed dissenters—from the Puritans who could not worship as they wished in the seventeenth century to the Hungarians who fled here after their country's revolt against the Russians in 1956. The country had embraced them all. Shouldn't it now embrace its own dissenting sons?

To Heal a Wound

Practically all who favored amnesty (again, conditional as well as unconditional) saw it as the only means for quickly and decisively healing the national wounds caused by the desertions and evasions. They prophesied that, without it, there would be endless years of prosecutions and retributions as the deserters and evaders drifted back home one by one. An upheaval that might otherwise soon be forgotten as new events crowded it from mind would linger on interminably, damaging the quality of American life all the while. Good minds would be lost to the country. Families would remain unsettled, worried over the fate of a son. Time that could be better spent on more valuable legal projects would be given to the prosecuting and defending of each man. Critics of the United States would have a decades-long field day claiming that the nation was vindictive and lacking compassion.

Legal Evasion

Many who sought full amnesty felt that it was wrong to single out just the deserters and evaders for punishment. Millions of other Americans had deliberately avoided making any sacrifice. The reference here was to all the young men who had hidden behind their draft deferments or had played games with their draft boards. They, too, had evaded the service—the only difference being that they had done so legally.

Alfred B. Fitt wrote of their number in an article, "Amnesty," which appeared in *The New York Times Magazine* of September 8, 1974. Mr. Fitt was an Assistant Secretary of Defense in the administration of Lyndon B. Johnson.

He pointed out that the draft age in the 1960s ran from eighteen to twenty-six years, but that the men inducted came principally from the younger end of the range. Mainly, they were those "who turned 18 between July, 1963, and July, 1971. . . .

"There were 14.5 million of them, and of these 58 percent never served a day of active duty. Less than 12 percent was drafted. Fewer than one in three volunteered. Of the six million who did serve, only about a third actually went to Vietnam—or one out of seven in the total manpower pool of the Vietnam war years. The other 8.5 million escaped service in a variety of ways."

Admittedly, many were exempted or deferred from service for valid reasons, but many "simply stayed in college and graduate school long enough to turn 26 and thus end their draft liability. The rise in college attendance was extraordinary—among males: 29 percent of 18- and 19-year-old American boys were in college in 1963; the rate increased by more than a third, to 39 percent, by 1969. It has since fallen back to 35 percent. No such surge occurred in the college attendance of 18- and 19-year-old girls. The conclusion is inescapable that the draft and the war propelled hundreds of thousands of young men into college during 1965 to 1970 who would not otherwise have attended."

Echoing the words of the Californian in Chapter 4, Mr. Fitt then wrote that many men avoided service by playing games with their draft boards. In the first five years of the 1960s, he reported, there were 41,462 appeals to draft board decisions. In the second five years, the figure jumped to an astonishing 596,258.

Further, he contended that, "in numbers which defy estimation, men escaped the draft through corrupt means. Some evaders found physicians, either venal or passionately opposed to the war, who would conspire with them to create false or dubious disqualifying medical histories. Some men bribed their way into reserve units. Some pretended homosexuality. Some ran away, not on moral grounds, but simply out of fear."

In the light of such accusations as these, many advocates of amnesty felt it unjust to punish those who had acted honestly by coming out in the open with their refusal to participate in the war.

No Amnesty

The basic argument against any amnesty at all held that, in a democracy, a man is guaranteed the right to oppose the enactment of laws and to oppose those already on the books. But he must always act within the framework of the nation's legal and social order, drawing sufficient people to his view to justify a change. If he cannot do this for any reason, he then has the right to disobey the laws involved. But he then must be prepared to face the consequences of his act. If he is unwilling to face them, he has no choice but to leave the country and its jurisdiction.

This, the no-amnesty supporters felt, was the exact position in which the deserters and evaders had placed themselves. If the war and the draft had truly outraged their consciences and they had felt unable to influence a change in government policy before being called to the fighting, then they had exercised a legitimate option in fleeing. But they must now face the authorities, tell their side of the story, and accept whatever punishment was given them. To grant them amnesty, to let them off free, would be to violate the country's legal and social order.

But what of the people in the antiwar movement who claimed that the United States, in pursuing the war against a rising tide of contrary public opinion, had lost its status as a democracy and had become a totalitarian state in which a man could not exercise his right to work for a change in the law? He was then, in effect, a "political prisoner." He had the right to rebel in any way possible. Was there any substance to this view?

As the advocates of no-amnesty saw the matter, the answer was "no." They argued that, on several counts, the country had remained a democracy throughout the entire Vietnam era.

First, the government had never throttled the war debate. The press had reported on all aspects of the controversy. Both ardent support for and harsh criticism against our Vietnam involvement had been found in newspapers, magazines, and books, and on radio and television. Despite official efforts to hide certain bleak facts about the war, there had never been here those hallmarks of the totalitarian state—over-all censorship or a government take-over of the press.

Further, in an era of violent demonstrations, the government had not deprived citizens of their right to assemble peaceably to air their views. It was true that police and, at times, military units had been on hand at campus and street demonstrations. But their function had not been to squash dissent but to protect surrounding life and property and to maintain or restore order. And it was true that some demonstrations had been dispersed, but they had been assemblies judged dangerous to public safety or contrary to long-standing law. And true that the police and troops had clashed with the demonstrators, but they had done so in the face of impending or actual violence. And so it could be said with reasonable safety that the right of Americans to assemble, legally and peaceably, had never been seriously threatened.

Most no-amnesty proponents would agree that the government had strained citizen rights in several areas. There had been, for example, instances of government surveillance of antiwar groups—*spying* was the popular word used to describe it. And there had been official lies about military and political conditions in Vietnam. And, especially during Mr. Nixon's administration, efforts had been made to coerce the news media into seeing things the government's way. None of these measures had been in the best of the democratic tradition. Each was to be feared, deplored, and guarded against in the future. But, the no-amnesty people contended, none had squashed the opposition. None had escaped open, public discussion and criticism. While assuredly soiling the country's democratic fabric, none had so destroyed it that the nation had been sent down the drain to totalitarianism.

Finally, the no-amnesty people argued, the government had responded to the public disenchantment with Vietnam. The draft law had been changed, and then, a short time later, the draft had been dropped altogether. U.S. troops had been brought home, and Congress had decreed that the President could send no forces there in the future without its consent. Granted, a number of factors other than public discontent had played a part in the troops' departure; involved were such factors as the war's economic drain on the country and the realization that the fighting could drag on for years without a clear-cut victory. But there is no doubt that public discontent much accounted for the withdrawal. In responding to that discontent as it did, the government was behaving not as a government in a totalitarian state but as one in a democracy.

And so, in all, despite all the clashes and despite the actions of some government leaders, the democratic tradition had remained intact in the United States throughout the Vietnam era. The deserters and evaders could not now demand amnesty on the grounds that they had been living in a totalitarian state and so were entitled to battle it in any way available to them. They had now to risk the punishment that was the right of the country to seek.

From these beginning no-amnesty arguments, let us now turn to others.

A Basic Offense

In addition to breaking the law, the deserters and evaders had committed another basic offense. They had turned their backs on the nation in a time of trial.

In the matter of abandoning the country in a time of need, the proponents of no-amnesty argued that military action and strength are necessary tools for any nation. With them, the nation is able to carry out many of its policies and defend itself. When a young man flees from military service in a time of crisis, he strikes directly at the country's ability to further those policies and protect itself. The refusal or the desertion of one man may not have serious consequences. But what if the number of men is great? Then the consequences can be grave, even disastrous. For then the country's policies and defense may not be the only factors at stake. At stake also may be its very survival.

Admittedly, the number of deserters and evaders did not cripple the Vietnam military effort or endanger this country's survival. But the potential for great damage was present—and so the offense must be regarded as inexcusable. Further, there is the future to consider. If pardon were granted the deserters and evaders, a dangerous precedent would be set. In future times of crisis, many men, knowing they would not be punished, might refuse service—

so many, in fact, that the country's survival might indeed be jeopardized.

Legal War

A number of the points made by the no-amnesty supporters were replies to views coming from the people favoring amnesty.

For instance, there was the response to the argument that the deserters and evaders should be pardoned because the war had been illegal. The no-amnesty people admitted that Congress had not issued a formal declaration of war, but they pointed to the fact that Congress consistently appropriated funds for the Vietnam effort. This financial support, they said, legitimatized the war quite as much as a formal declaration would have.

A separate point was leveled against the evaders. The obligation to serve in the military had never been contingent on a declared war. The draft had been in effect during many a peacetime year, and the call to duty had been obeyed by thousands of young men.

The Nuremberg Principle

Many of the people who favored amnesty believed that U.S. forces, especially in their bombings and napalm attacks, had been guilty of "crimes against humanity" in the Vietnam fighting. The deserters and evaders, they contended, should be amnestied because they had refused to participate in those crimes. The refusal had been in keeping with the international law known as the "Nuremberg principle."

The principle had been established at Nuremberg, Germany, during the post–World War II trials of Nazi leaders. It maintained that the agent of a sovereign state could be held personally responsible for any brutal acts—any "crimes against humanity"—which he committed as part of his wartime duties, even if he committed them on the instructions of his superiors. Previously, he had escaped punishment for brutalities committed on the orders of superiors.

The no-amnesty people replied that the Nuremberg principle could not be applied to the deserters and evaders. First, in the past, it had been directed only against the agents of a defeated power—and the United States, though it had withdrawn from Vietnam, could not be considered a defeated nation. Second, the question of "crimes against humanity" was a matter of debate. The American people, as a whole, had never determined that the U.S. forces had been guilty of such acts. Until such a determination was made, there were no grounds for invoking the Nuremberg principle.

Guessing Games—a Fallacy

A mainstay argument for amnesty was that the deserters and evaders had done no more than prematurely resist a war that the rest of the country had eventually come to see as evil. They had defied laws supporting a government policy that had later been reversed. Theirs was a wisdom that should not be punished.

William A. Rusher, the publisher of *National Review* magazine, replied to the argument. Writing in the book *Amnesty: The Unsettled Question of Vietnam,* he commented:

"Virtually every law is likely to be repealed, or at least fall into desuetude, sooner or later. Citizens must not be encouraged to play guessing games with the state—betting that a given policy will be reversed, violating its legal supports in that cheerful faith, and then living abroad, or incognito, until a reversal occurs, only to emerge triumphant and unpunishable when amnesty is proclaimed. . . .

"No society could survive a month if everyone who correctly predicted the subsequent reversal of specific governmental policies went unpunished for violating the laws that implemented them."

Further, Mr. Rusher argued, there had never been a "clear-cut reversal" of America's Vietnam policy. Granted, aid was given in increasing amounts during the Kennedy and Johnson administrations, after which Mr. Nixon had begun the troop withdrawal. But the South Vietnamese Army had not been strong enough to defend its country during the Kennedy and Johnson administrations, and Mr. Nixon had spent several years bringing it to the point where it could stand by itself before beginning the withdrawal. His actions, then, did not constitute a reversal of U.S. policy, but rather the slow evolvement of that policy to a new, though different, level. Consequently, the deserters and evaders could not be said to be resisting a policy that was reversed. They were, instead, defying the nation's evolving policy.

A Historical Precedent

Still another major amnesty argument held that the deserters and evaders should be excused because the nation had long ago set a precedent for granting amnesties.

The no-amnesty supporters sharply disagreed, despite the fact that thirty-four amnesties had been declared in U.S. history. What was being sought by the full-amnesty people, they said, was a general amnesty for wartime deserters and evaders. No such sweeping amnesty had ever been granted in U.S. history. There was no precedent for awarding one now.

All past amnesties, they argued, had been of a limited and specific nature. They had been granted to a handful of farmers in the Whiskey Insurrection; to Confederate sympathizers, but always with exceptions, in the Civil War; and to only about 10 percent of the men who had evaded the draft in World War II. The only universal amnesty proclaimed in United States history—Andrew Johnson's amnesty of Christmas Day, 1868—had been effectively nullified by Congress.

Further, most amnesties granted for desertion had been for peacetime desertions. There had been amnesties for wartime desertions, yes, but they had customarily carried penalties, such as a return to duty and a forfeiture of pay for the time absent.

There was no historical precedent whatsoever for granting a general unconditional amnesty today.

Conditional Amnesty

The Americans who favored conditional amnesty took a middle-of-the-road position.

They were people of divided opinion. In common with their countrymen who argued for full amnesty, they viewed the deserters and evaders sympathetically, and the war as either a tragic mistake or a legitimate enterprise that had nevertheless tragically split the nation. But, as did those who opposed any sort of amnesty, they recognized that the young men had broken the law and that, if all law was to continue to have any meaning in the United States, they could not be excused without punishment.

Further, they realized how high public feeling was running over the amnesty issue. A decision for unconditional amnesty or for no amnesty at all was bound to outrage one segment of the public or the other. The whole controversy would not be ended but rather intensified, perhaps with tragic consequences.

And so they urged a compromise, a conditional amnesty. It would not punish the deserters and evaders with something as harsh as a prison sentence or a stiff fine. But it would not let them go completely free either. It would forget what they had done only after they had met certain conditions imposed by the government.

It was this middle-of-the-road approach that President Gerald Ford chose when, in 1974, he entered the amnesty debate and offered his "program of reconciliation," as he called it, to the deserters and evaders. More of that program in the next chapters.

As the amnesty debate gained momentum, it was joined by various public figures and organizations.

Among the first national figures to make their views known were senators Eugene McCarthy and Edward Kennedy, and Congressman Edward I. Koch. During his 1968 presidential campaign, Senator McCarthy, long a foe of the Vietnam involvement, remarked that he favored a "kind of amnesty" but did not go into specifics. Next, in 1969, Senator Kennedy authored a bill that revised the Selective Service laws; he recommended a study "to determine the appropriateness of granting amnesty in the near future" to men "outside the United States who are liable for prosecution"; the bill was defeated. Then Congressman Koch, in a move that did not concern amnesty directly but still had a similar meaning, presented a bill that would redefine conscientious objection.

Congressman Koch sought to have conscientious objection broadened to include selective objection to *particular wars* on the basis of conscience. He asked that all the resisters now in jail, in the military, on the run, or in foreign countries be allowed to apply for CO status under the proposed redefinition.

When presenting his bill, Mr. Koch told his fellow legislators that he was not offering the deserters and evaders an amnesty but a "second chance":

"I am introducing a bill today that would provide a second chance to those young men who have been opposed to participation in the Vietnam war and yet have been forced into the heartrending dilemma of service in a war they oppose or prison or flight from the country. By second chance, I mean giving a young man the opportunity now to offer information to his local board in substantiation of his claim to exemption from military service, provided he was conscientiously opposed to participation in a particular war at the time he received a notice to report for induction or at the time he left a jurisdiction to evade military service."

Nothing came of the Koch bill. It was sent to the House Committee on Armed Services, where it languished for more than a year and a half. But Congressman Koch could take solace in the fact that each passing month heard new and influential voices joining in the call for amnesty. Among them was that of the late Richard Cardinal Cushing. In his 1970 address at Eastertime, the Catholic prelate suggested the idea of amnesty when he said:

"Would it be too much to suggest that this Easter we . . . call back from over the border and around the world the young men who are called deserters? Perhaps this year we should dramatize this notion of beginning, of newness, by doing something unprecedented in our life as a nation."

The organizations that joined in the debate were many. Practically every religious denomination in the country spoke out in favor of one kind of amnesty or another. Among the religious organizations that made their feelings known were the American Baptist Church, the American Lutheran Church, the Episcopal Church, the American Jewish Congress, the National Conference of Catholic Bishops, and the National Council of Churches of Christ.

They all issued formal statements on their positions on amnesty. Each statement, of course, represented each organization's view. But they all shared much the same sentiment. Representative of the feelings of the American religious community was the position taken by the United Church of Christ. At its Seventh General Synod, held in mid-1969, the church declared:

"In the interests of reconciliation and the binding up of wounds, for the sake of our freedoms and to allow our high respect for conscience, in the best tradition of a strong and secure democracy, in the name of Christian love, we urge the President of the United States to grant, at the earliest possible opportunity, amnesty and pardon for those who for actions witnessing to their beliefs have been incarcerated, deprived of their rights of citizenship, or led by their conscience into exile during the course of the nation's great agony in the Vietnam war. We urge these bold actions because this nation needs, and is strong enough to embrace, both those who have engaged in the Vietnam conflict and those who have opposed it."

Also joining in the call for amnesty were such organizations as the Southern Christian Leadership Conference, which the late Martin Luther King had once headed; the Clergy and Laity Concerned, a national interfaith group of churchmen and laymen; Americans for Amnesty, a group consisting of citizens from all walks of life; and the Vietnam Veterans Against the War, an organization of men who had served in Vietnam and had come to oppose the American involvement there. In the organization were men who had been discharged from the service and men who were still in uniform.

One of the most influential of the organizations seeking amnesty was the American Civil Liberties Union (ACLU). A nationwide organization some fifty years old, it is dedicated to protecting and preserving the individual rights of any American whenever they are threatened. It now demanded unconditional amnesty and established Project on Amnesty, a unit that was to devote its full attention to pressing home that demand.

The ACLU urged amnesty not just for the deserters and evaders. It wanted an unconditional amnesty for *all* men whose attitudes had run them afoul of the military during the war. Such an amnesty would embrace countless men. It would include the thousands who had received service discharges in the less-than-honorable categories for "poor" attitudes, misbehavior, and offenses connected with a dislike of the war or the armed services. And it would remove from the less-than-honorable-discharge ranks the thousands more whom the military had dismissed as incompetent, unstable, or undesirable; included here were men who had been discharged for below-par intelligence, for uncooperative attitudes, for drug usage, for homosexual tendencies, and even for bed-wetting. As the ACLU saw it, the draft had forced all these unfortunates into the service, and then the Army had kicked them back out and, with the less-than-honorable discharges, had labeled them as misfits because it did not like them or did not want to work with them.

The ACLU held that everyone—from the deserters and evaders to the misfits—had suffered a violation of their civil rights. Because of a war that they neither wanted nor understood, they were now burdened with a stigma that might damage the quality of their lives for years to come. It could earn them the open contempt of many of their fellow citizens, reduce their chances for getting jobs, and make it difficult for them to obtain business permits and even driver's licenses. There was only one way to correct the whole situation quickly. An unconditional amnesty that blanketed them all must be granted.

The Americans for Amnesty agreed with the ACLU, saying that some 450,000 men had been saddled with undesirable and less-than-honorable discharges. It further pointed out that these men deserved an unconditional amnesty because the section of military law under which the discharges had been issued had recently been judged "unconstitutionally vague" by a federal court.

Now what of the public figures and organizations on the opposite side of the fence? President Richard M. Nixon led this list of individuals. Though he had been the one to order U.S. troops home, he was adamantly opposed to amnesty. He regarded the deserters and evaders as lawbreakers. Throughout his stay in the White House he was on record as saying, "Amnesty means forgiveness. We cannot provide forgiveness for them."

Further, at a press conference some months before his resignation, he remarked: "Those who served paid their price. Those who deserted must pay their price, and the price is not a junket in the

Peace Corps, or something like that, as some have suggested. The price is a criminal penalty for disobeying the laws of the United States. If they return to the United States, they must pay the price."

Siding with Mr. Nixon were many government and military officials. They were joined by such organizations as the American Legion, whose membership is made up principally of men who have fought in the two world wars and in Korea; the Non-Commissioned Officers Association, made up of veterans and servicemen below the rank of lieutenant and above that of private; and the Veterans of Foreign Wars, consisting of former servicemen whose tours of duty have taken them overseas.

And what of the men in the middle—the deserters and evaders? Newspaper reports held that most of them wanted nothing to do with amnesty if it involved the slightest hint of forgiveness. They were convinced that they had done what was morally right, and had done so at great sacrifice. And so, as one said, "There's nothing to be forgiven for."

Another, quoted in the January 17, 1972, issue of *Newsweek* magazine, remarked: "It makes me sad to think that people in the States are working hard to get amnesty, because people up here [Canada] aren't going to appreciate it, especially if there is some notion that we have to admit guilt. There is no guilt up here."

Others felt that the nation's leaders had behaved criminally in pursuing an undeclared and immoral war. Said one deserter in Toronto, Canada: "Punish them. Or forgive them. Whichever you choose. But not us."

In particular, the talk of amnesty struck hard at the pride of many deserters and evaders. *The New York Post,* in a January 1973 edition, reported one exile in Canada as saying: "Amnesty be damned. . . . The pompous American attitude that all war resisters just spend their time gazing longingly over the border, aching to live down there again, makes me sick." In Sweden, another exile said that he would probably come home if granted unconditional amnesty. "But," he added, "I don't think we committed any crimes, and I'm not going to crawl and beg."

Regardless of such attitudes, the amnesty debate continued to rage, attracting more and more people as time passed. In May of

1973, barely four months after the last American combat units had departed Vietnam, a National Conference on Amnesty drew several hundred people to Washington, D.C., for discussions on the need for amnesty. Then, for three days in March 1974, the House Judiciary Subcommittee on Courts, Civil Liberties and the Administration of Justice met to take testimony on all aspects of the debate. Altogether, thirty-two witnesses appeared before the subcommittee. Here are samplings of what was said:

Senator Ernest Gruening urged a full and immediate amnesty for all deserters and evaders. Further, he called on the government to apologize to them. He said that the amnesty should be accompanied by a "declaration of appreciation for their decency and humanitarianism." With Senator Wayne Morse, Gruening had been the only man in the Senate to vote against the Gulf of Tonkin Resolution back in 1964.

Speaking of the deserters, he won a burst of applause from the pro-amnesty members of the audience when he said: "Their deserting was infinitely preferable to continuing as killers and maimers of a people against whom the U.S. had no grievance whatsoever."

Among those who testified on behalf of conditional amnesty was Senator Robert Taft, Jr., of Ohio. He recommended that a review board be established to look into the cases of draft evasion. The board could allow the charges against an evader to be dropped if he agreed to serve up to two years in public service work, perhaps in a hospital or with an organization such as VISTA. Senator Taft had embodied this idea in a bill that he had prepared for Senate consideration. The bill contained no mention of deserters, for the offense of running away after one was in uniform was considered far more serious than draft evasion.

Robert Froehlke, the Secretary of the Army under President Nixon during the war, advised that the cases of those who deserted out of hatred for the war be reviewed, with pardons being granted as warranted. Mr. Froehlke had supported the government's policy while the fighting was still in progress, but now he asked that the draft evaders be amnestied. He said that amnesty would help mend "the heartbreak and wounds left by the war."

Echoing President Nixon's no-amnesty sentiments, a representative of the Non-Commissioned Officers Association said: "These men are criminals. Their refusal to be drafted or to go into or remain in combat caused others to be drafted and sent into combat as their replacements and possibly wounded, maimed, or killed. The good God calls upon us for mercy, but He did not mention amnesty."

And what of those who had "to serve in the place" of the deserters and evaders? What of *all* who had served? What of their families? How would they feel were an amnesty granted? Walter Morse, a general counsel for the Selective Service System, prophesied a molten anger among them all. Just as the resisters had been a divisive element in the country during the war, he said, so now the veterans, their families, and the families of those who had died would become the divisive element. Amnesty would not, contrary to the hopes of its advocates, reunite the nation. It would only split it again.

The hearings did not produce any legislative advice from the subcommittee, for they were held primarily to hear various shades of opinion that might prove useful at a later date. The subcommittee chairman, Representative Robert Kastenmeier, admitted that the nation was a great distance from a solution of the problem and that there would need to be "some changes of heart" on the parts of many before any solution could be considered. But the hearings were responsible for one accomplishment: they enabled the American public, in a matter of just three days, to hear all sides of the amnesty debate.

Then, just six months later, the public was given a possible solution to the whole problem. On taking office, President Ford proposed a program for the deserters and evaders, one that, as he put it, would welcome them back to the mainstream of American life.

7

THE FORD PROGRAM

President Ford's announcement of his amnesty program came as no surprise to the American people that morning of September 16, 1974. They knew that he had been working on the program for several weeks. Its announcement had originally been scheduled for earlier in the month, but had been called off after Mr. Ford had pardoned Richard Nixon of any criminal charges that might arise out of the Watergate scandal and be leveled against the just-resigned President.

Branding the pardon unfair, large segments of the public reacted so angrily that Mr. Ford delayed the amnesty announcement "indefinitely" to allow tempers to cool before he broached another controversial issue. But reaction to the delay had been equally sharp, with many people asking how the administration dared to leave all the evaders and deserters "hanging in the balance" after settling one man's future so quickly. And so there had been a change of heart in the White House, and the announcement had followed within a few days.

Nor did the nature of the Ford program itself surprise anyone. It was a compromise, one that fell midway between unconditional amnesty and no amnesty at all. Americans everywhere had expected that, for in late August they had heard the new President express his views on amnesty. Addressing a Chicago convention of the Veterans of Foreign Wars, he had called himself a long-time opponent of any "unconditional blanket amnesty" for those who "evaded or fled military service." But, he had added, the time was at hand "to bind up the wounds of the nation."

This, the President felt, could be done with a program that would permit the evaders and deserters "to work their way back home" if they so desired. He wanted to see them back home so that they would "have a second chance to contribute their fair share to the rebuilding of peace among ourselves and with all nations." The program that he had in mind—and that was now being developed with the assistance of Attorney General William Saxbe and Secretary of Defense James Schlesinger—would provide that chance by allowing them to perform tasks of benefit to the public.

Mr. Ford promised that, in the program, he would throw "the weight of my presidency into the scales of U.S. justice on the side of leniency." He promised not to seek revenge with the program but to act "promptly, fairly, and firmly in the same spirit that guided Abraham Lincoln and Harry Truman."

When he at last announced the work program, he offered it to evaders and deserters who were still at large, and to those who had earlier surrendered to or had been caught by military authorities. The latter category included those who had been convicted or otherwise punished for their offenses and those who still awaited trial or sentencing. Excluded, however, was any convicted man who was also serving time for some other criminal offense.

When announcing the program, Mr. Ford did not describe it as one offering amnesty. Rather, he called it a program of "earned reentry to the mainstream of American society." Not once did he use the term *amnesty*, and there can be no doubt that he avoided it because it is so charged with emotion and controversy. But there can also be no doubt that, by whatever name it is called, the program offered conditional amnesty. It was based on two conditions set down by Mr. Ford. Only if the evaders and deserters agreed to both would the memory of their offenses be dismissed.

The conditions were:

1. The deserters and evaders had to consent to do up to twenty-four months in public service work that the government called "reconciliation service" but that was more popularly known as "alternative service." Such work was intended to take the place of military duty or any fines or prison sentences that might otherwise be imposed. The jobs that could be taken as alternative service were many. They ranged from those as hospital attendants and orderlies to those as workers with public service organizations (VISTA, Goodwill Industries, etc.), ecological projects, and church groups dedicated to the public good. They were to be paying jobs, but, because of their nature, their pay was to be low.

The President stipulated that the twenty-four-month work period was to be a maximum one. It could be reduced, he explained, in any case where "mitigating circumstances" showed themselves. Examples of mitigating circumstances were poor health or family hardship.

2. Certain of the evaders and deserters were to sign their names to documents reaffirming their allegiance to the United States and pledging to do the twenty-four months of alternative service. This condition applied only to those evaders and deserters who had not yet been convicted for their offenses.

For those men who had already been convicted or otherwise punished, Mr. Ford established what he called the Presidential Clemency Board. Its job was to review their cases and make recommendations as to what should be done about them. Some men might be completely pardoned. Some might be returned to prison. Others might be made to do alternative service.

The President appointed former Senator Charles E. Goodell of New York to be chairman of the Clemency Board. Named as members were Ralph Adams, president of Alabama's Troy State University; James P. Dougovita, a teacher at Michigan Technological University and a Vietnam veteran; Robert H. Finch, former Secretary of Health, Education, and Welfare; the Reverend Theodore Hesburgh, president of the University of Notre Dame; Vernon E. Jordan, executive director of the National Urban League; James Maye, executive director of the Paralyzed Veterans of America; Aida C. O'Connor, assistant counsel to the New York Division of Housing and

Community Renewal; and General Lewis W. Walt, a retired assistant commandant of the Marine Corps.

Two conditions and a Presidential Clemency Board—these constituted the principal features of the Ford program. In a moment, we'll look at the program in detail. But, first, two questions need to be asked. Who exactly would be eligible for the program? How many men would be involved?

The first question is difficult to answer. The program covered so many men and such a variety of offenses that eligibility was always a matter of confusion. In general, however, the men could be divided into five classes:

1. *Unconvicted Evaders*: In this class were all men who had yet to be tried for evasion. Included were evaders under indictment and those still at large, whether living openly abroad or hiding out here at home.

2. *Convicted Evaders*: These men had already been tried and found guilty of violating the Selective Service Act. Their offenses included draft card burning, the refusal to be inducted, and evasion.

3. *Unconvicted Deserters*: Classed here were all deserters yet to be tried. Eligible were men at large and men already in custody and awaiting trial. The charges against them ranged from desertion to being absent without official leave. (As mentioned earlier, absence without official leave—AWOL—is the charge for an unauthorized absence of less than thirty days; desertion is the charge for an unauthorized absence exceeding thirty days.)

4. *Convicted Deserters*: Here were all men who had been tried successfully. In common with the unconvicted deserters, their offenses ranged from desertion to being AWOL.

5. *Certain Veterans*: This class was made up of men who held less-than-honorable discharges for such violations as desertion or being AWOL.

Now, what of the number of men possibly involved? An overall total is impossible to come by, for the exact number of men who evaded the draft without being detected was unknown—and remains unknown to this day. No one knew, for instance, how many men had won 4-F classifications with faked medical records. Nor did anyone know how many thousands had evaded the draft simply by failing to register for it on turning eighteen years of age. All, if caught, were liable for prosecution and thus perhaps eligible for the program.

Even the figures for known or suspected offenders were far from definite. Totals were computed by various organizations at the time, but they varied greatly, usually according to where the organizations' sympathies lay. Full-amnesty groups came up with totals on the high side, while the government and no-amnesty supporters were inclined to more conservative estimates. The reasons for the discrepancies were at least two. First, to strengthen their respective positions, one side tended to maximize the size of the problem and the other to minimize it. Second, the figures reflected each side's ideas of exactly who should be included in the program.

Consequently, a total, accurate and agreeable to all, is impossible to determine. The best that can be done is to compare two representative sets of opposing figures and hope that a reasonable estimate emerges. The figures used here come from the government and the Americans for Amnesty organization.

In statistics that accompanied President Ford's announcement, government sources estimated that the program would involve at *least* 29,000 men—approximately 15,500 evaders and 13,100 deserters. Of the evader total, around 8,700 men had already been convicted for their offenses, while another 4,350 were under indictment, and yet another 2,250 under investigation. Out of all those who had been convicted, 130 were still serving their prison sentences. Of the 4,350 under indictment, 4,060 were listed as fugitives, with more than 3,000 said to be living abroad.

As was said earlier, about 90 percent of all the men who deserted during the Vietnam years had returned voluntarily or had been apprehended, with their cases then being settled in one way or another. Further cases had been disposed of in the time since, and the government now estimated that the fate of roughly 13,100 deserters had yet to be fully resolved. Of that number, about 12,500 were fugitives, with around 1,500 of their number known to be living abroad. Another 660 were serving prison sentences or awaiting trial.

To the government total the Presidential Clemency Board added approximately 120,000. The board estimated this to be the number of convicted evaders and deserters who might be eligible to have it review their cases. Altogether, then, the government total came to a minimum of 149,000 men.

The Americans for Amnesty organization used figures from both government and independent sources to compile its totals. The totals came out looking like this:

There were a known 52,143 draft resisters from the war years. Of their number, 7,443 had been convicted, with 3,666 being imprisoned for up to five years. Another 5,700 still faced outstanding indictments and possible punishment. Altogether, 39,000 names had been filed with the Department of Justice as Selective Service violators.

Additionally, the Americans for Amnesty said that the Pentagon had 32,557 men listed as "at large" for desertion and for being AWOL.

As was said in the preceding chapter, the Americans for Amnesty agreed with the ACLU's stand that some 450,000 young Americans needed to be freed of those less-than-honorable discharges that had been given them for such reasons as incompetency, instability, behavioral problems, and drug usage. The organization added them to its totals.

In all, the Americans for Amnesty figures indicated that as many as 534,700 Americans were in need of amnesty—a total that exceeded the government's by more than 385,000 men.

And, the organization added, the total would climb to even greater heights should the young men who had avoided the draft by faking medical records or failing to register be apprehended.

Now for the details of the program:

President Ford announced that the program would apply only to those men whose desertions and evasions had occurred in the eight-and-a-half-year period between August 4, 1964, and March 28, 1973—the period between the date on which the Senate ratified the Gulf of Tonkin Resolution and the day on which the last U.S. combat units departed Vietnam. He gave all eligible men until January 31, 1975, to enroll in the program.

Then he placed the running of the program with four governmental bodies—the newly formed Presidential Clemency Board, the Department of Defense, the Department of Justice, and the

Selective Service System. Assigned to each were the following men and responsibilities:

1. *Presidential Clemency Board*: The board was to handle three categories of offender: (A) all convicted evaders, (B) all convicted deserters, and (C) all veterans holding less-than-honorable discharges on such counts as desertion and being AWOL. It was to review their cases and then make three recommendations to the President.

First, it was to recommend whether a man in category A or B was to be shown clemency—that is, pardoned. Second, it was to recommend whether a man in category C was to have his less-than-honorable discharge replaced with one thought to be less damaging to his future, one that was to be called a "clemency discharge." Third, it was to recommend whether a man in category B also was deserving of a clemency discharge.

Finally, in any of its recommendations, the board could set certain requirements concerning the twenty-four months of alternative service work. It could determine whether the full twenty-four-month period or some portion of it was to be served. As the President had announced, the length of service would depend greatly on mitigating circumstances.

2. *Department of Defense*: Assigned to the Department of Defense were all unconvicted deserters. They were told that their cases would be handled at Camp Atterbury (later, at Fort Benjamin Harrison), Indiana. There they would be given an "undesirable discharge" in exchange for signing a reaffirmation of allegiance to the country and a pledge to perform up to twenty-four months in an alternative service job. Upon completion of their alternate service, they would have their undesirable discharges replaced with clemency discharges.

As did the Clemency Board, the department had the authority to reduce the term of alternative service if mitigating circumstances so warranted.

3. *Department of Justice*: Responsibility for handling all unconvicted evaders went to the Department of Justice. These men were to surrender themselves to a local United States attorney's office, where they were to sign two documents—one the pledge to do

alternative service, the other a waiver of certain rights. (The rights involved will be discussed in the next chapter.) Contained within their pledge was an implied reaffirmation of their allegiance to the country.

Once the men had completed their alternative service, the department would drop their cases, agreeing never to prosecute them for draft violations. The department had the right to reduce terms of alternative service in the presence of mitigating circumstances.

4. *Selective Service System*: The SSS was assigned the task of administering the alternative service work program. Each man was to find his own job, but the SSS was to keep tabs on him and then, at the end of his work term, was to certify that he had successfully fulfilled his obligation. Once the certification was made, the final terms of his clemency would be granted the man.

When announcing the plan, Mr. Ford stressed that it was being offered in mercy and as a means of reconciliation between all the young men and the nation. He said:

"Desertion in the time of war is a major, serious offense; failure to respond to the country's call of duty is also a serious offense. . . . Reconciliation among our people does not require that these acts be condoned. . . . Yet reconciliation calls for an act of mercy to bind up the wounds of the nation and heal the scars of divisiveness."

Now, with the word of the program flashing across the country, two questions had to be uppermost in his mind:

Though this "act of mercy," this means of reconciliation, was a compromise, would it nevertheless win enough support among the young men and the general public to be a success? Would it end the amnesty problem?

Within hours of the announcement, the President began to get the answers.

The program was in trouble.

THE BIOGRAPHY OF
A PROGRAM

There was bound to be trouble. The White House knew that the unconditional amnesty groups would never accept the program. Nor would the most stubborn of the deserters and evaders. Nor the no-amnesty people. The unconditional amnesty groups and the men would settle for nothing less than full vindication, while the no-amnesty people would go on calling for punishment.

But there was hope that the program would appeal to others. It might win favor among conditional amnesty supporters, and among large segments of the public eager to be rid of the Vietnam controversy. Most important of all, many of the deserters and evaders might find it acceptable. Their wish to be home and to get on with their lives might outweigh their desire for full amnesty.

The program, for instance, seemed to offer the conditional amnesty people just what they were asking for. Here was amnesty with some provisos attached—provisos that, hopefully, would be seen as just but not too harsh. As for the general public, a recent opinion poll had indicated that most Americans were coming to favor conditional amnesty, at least for the evaders. Between March 29 and April 1, 1974, the Gallup organization had interviewed 1,537 adults in three hundred different localities on the evader question. Of the people surveyed, 58 percent said that the young men should not be allowed to return without some form of punishment, while 38 percent favored unconditional amnesty. Further, more than four out of five in the 58 percent came out against seeing the evaders fined or imprisoned. They believed that a period of time served in the armed forces or in a nonmilitary service organization such as VISTA would suffice. Only 6 percent of the interviewees favored imprisonment. A scant 2 percent wanted a fine.

Too, there could even be hope that some people in the no-amnesty camp might be starting to change their minds. In a *New York Times* article, written shortly after the Ford announcement, reporter Jon Nordheimer caught a beginning shift of attitude among the members of the American Legion post at Ventura, California. Most of the members still clung to their long-standing opposition to amnesty. But two comments were at odds with the general feeling.

One came from a World War II Seabee: "My position has changed completely on Vietnam. In the beginning I was against every long-hair S.O.B., but now I've got to admire people who went to jail to protest the war. They made us pay attention to what was happening. The way I feel now I'd stand up for a man who opposed it on moral grounds."

The second, voiced by an oil-field worker, centered itself on the pardon given former President Nixon in the Watergate scandal. Before that pardon, the man said, "There wasn't any way I'd let those guys come back, no sir, no way. But after Nixon I say the hell with it, there should be no way these kids should be punished and he gets away clean."

Just two comments, yes. But perhaps a reflection of a changing trend. A changing trend that might make the plan all the more acceptable to the public.

Finally, what of the deserters and evaders themselves? It was hoped that they would see the plan as a practical solution to their problem. Granted, they would have to work for up to two years in menial and low-paying jobs. But at least they would be free men in their own country while doing so. Wouldn't many find this preferable to languishing in jail or remaining at loose ends underground or in exile? Hopefully, many would consider the twenty-four months a fair trade for years of knowing they could not return home without facing prosecution. And, hopefully, many would see that the program, even though it offered much less than full amnesty, did represent a government shift from an earlier hard-line stand. Perhaps they would be willing to respond with a similar shift.

These hopes may have run high during the first hours after Mr. Ford's announcement. But they were dashed as soon as the first reactions started coming in. The program was branded as useless, poorly constructed, and dangerous. We need now look at each of these criticisms in turn, for they persisted through the next months and eventually condemned the program to failure.

The evaders and deserters immediately found the program not only useless but odious.

It did not, they charged, vindicate their sacrifices. Rather, by offering clemency, it implied that they were being forgiven for some wrong. "To accept the program would be an admission of guilt," said one American in Canada. "I feel that Ford's proposal will do more to split the country than to reunite it. I doubt seriously if many exiles will return after this."

Agreeing with him was a twenty-year-old evader living in Toronto. "It's very important that the lessons of resistance to the Vietnam war be learned and that we be vindicated. We owe this much to our people and our time."

Further, the exiles charged, the program not only failed to vindicate them but demanded that they sacrifice still more years of their lives. They had already lost much time. Now they were expected to give away another two years, this time in a menial, possibly fruitless labor.

One evader in Sweden called the alternative service work "penal servitude." He added hotly, "I'll be damned if I'll go back for something that's no better than a prison term. It's silly—stupid—to think that I would."

Many exiles felt insulted at the stipulation that they sign a reaffirmation of allegiance. "A signature on that reaffirmation would be self-incriminating," one said. "We'd be admitting that we'd been disloyal to the country. We weren't. We were warning the country that it was in trouble."

A friend added bluntly, "Ford must think we're pretty stupid to fall for that one."

Equally insulting, they felt, was the fact that the program was coming in the wake of Mr. Ford's pardon of former President Nixon. "Nixon goes scot-free after Watergate," one man in Canada grumbled. "But we get it in the neck."

Especially outraged was Amex, an organization of American exiles in Canada. The group called it "a gross miscarriage of justice for Nixon to get a pardon—plus a pension—for his very real crimes while war resisters are still punished."

Groups seeking unconditional amnesty shared the views of the exiles. Additionally, the groups dismissed the program as useless because it made no provision for all those 450,000 men who had received less-than-honorable discharges for such infractions as incompetence and instability. The stigma of their discharges had to be removed. The ACLU called the program "worse than no amnesty at all."

Now what of the criticism that the program was poorly constructed?

This criticism, which was soon echoed by Americans everywhere, was based mainly on one point. The program seemed to leave too many questions about its operation unanswered. They were questions that ranged from the very personal to the most general.

A man with a very personal question on his mind was a deserter living in Vancouver, British Columbia. He told *New York Times* reporter Jon Nordheimer that, before ever trying the program, he needed more information: "Like do they lock you up and make you wear a uniform and get a GI haircut?"

To which a companion added: "I'd take the haircut, but I'd be damned if I'd put that uniform on again."

Often-asked general questions dealt with apparent weaknesses in the program's workability. The young men were supposed to find alternative service jobs on their own. But what provision had been made against the possibility that there would not be enough jobs to go around? What would happen to a man who couldn't find a job—would he be amnestied or made to face prosecution? What if he found a job, grew tired of it, and quit? Under the terms of the program, would he be liable for prosecution? What of his work supervisor? What was *he* to do—keep his mouth shut, try to get the man back, or report him to the authorities? Wasn't all this putting an undue burden on an already busy supervisor; making a "policeman" of him when he had no desire to be one?

These were troublesome questions that many people thought should have been answered when the program was announced. Then, within a week or so after the announcement, public confidence in the thinking behind the program was further shaken. What quickly became known as the "deserter's loophole" was discovered.

The loophole was opened by a technicality in the procedure to be used by the Defense Department in handling unconvicted deserters. A man, remember, was to receive an undesirable discharge upon pledging to perform alternative service, and then was to have it replaced with a clemency discharge once he completed his term of work. But, it was quickly pointed out, as soon as he had the undesirable discharge in hand, he was a civilian again and thus beyond military control. If he was content to live with the undesirable discharge, he could end all his problems simply by refusing to do the two years of alternative service.

The loophole, which *Time* magazine termed an "incredible oversight," was sure to strike many an unconvicted deserter as an easy way out of his predicament. The undesirable discharge was little worse than the clemency discharge. Both denied him veteran's benefits, but neither legally barred him from general employment, though the former forbade work with the government. There was only one risk—that the government might prosecute a man for fraudulently signing the alternative service pledge just to obtain the undesirable discharge. To avoid two years of menial work, many deserters might think it a risk worth taking.

Now, to the dangers that many saw in the Ford plan: at the top of the list were the following:

Amnesty groups believed it unwise for a man to place himself in the hands of the government and sacrifice up to two years of his life for a clemency discharge. It was viewed as no better than those in the less-than-honorable categories, including the undesirable discharge. It carried with it a stigma that might hinder future career and social opportunities. It disqualified its owner from veteran's benefits. It very likely could not be reviewed if its owner someday wanted to have it changed.

Altogether—considering that a man would be open to prosecution and imprisonment if anything went wrong during his term of alternative service—he was risking too much for too little.

Those who were to be handled by the Presidential Clemency Board were risking even more. The amnesty groups reminded the men that there was no guarantee that they would be granted clemency at the end of their period of alternative service. The board was to make clemency recommendations to the President. But he need not automatically grant full clemency. For one reason or another he could decide not to expunge a man's record or clear him of all his liabilities.

Especially disliked by the amnesty groups was the provision that the evaders to be handled by the Department of Justice had to waive certain of their constitutional rights before being admitted to the program. To be waived away was the protection against draft prosecution under the statute of limitations, along with the right to an indictment, a speedy trial, and protection from double jeopardy. The groups warned that, were anything to go wrong after these rights had been waived, a man would have to face prosecution without any of the protections accorded to all defendants.

Further, the men were cautioned, the program contained no safeguards for the evader who applied to the department and then decided against signing the waiver. He risked being arrested on the spot. A department spokesman confirmed this point in an interview with United Press International. He said bluntly: "If a guy meets a U.S. attorney and won't sign the agreement, he would not be permitted to leave."

Equally disliked by many people was the length of time designated for alternative service. They thought it an unduly long period. Recent court decisions in evader cases gave credence to their feeling. In the early 1960s, the average sentence for a Selective Service violation was 37.3 months. But, by 1973, violators were receiving sentences that averaged 14.4 months before parole. In all, there was a difference of approximately ten months between the average draft sentence and the two-year maximum asked for alternative service.

Further, as the American Civil Liberties Union pointed out, nine out of every ten men whose names had gone to the Justice Department through the years for draft violations had never been indicted. There had been certain legal violations by the Selective Service System in the pursuit of their cases, violations that made convictions impossible. Of those who had been indicted, about two-thirds had seen their indictments dropped or had been acquitted by the courts.

All things considered, an evader might better end his problem by taking his case to court. He faced a danger, however. With the program, he was pretty much assured a pardon. By trying the courts, he might emerge a convicted felon, a label that would scar him for life.

Amnesty groups urged all unconvicted evaders to seek legal help and have their records thoroughly checked before ever applying for the program. A check might show that they had not actually violated the draft laws, or that their violations had not been formally noticed by the Selective Service System. If either was the case, they would have no need for the program.

The same advice went to all unconvicted deserters. A check of their records might show that they had good defenses against desertion charges. Those defenses might rise out of such factors as unlawful induction, medical problems, family hardship, and valid conscientious objection while in uniform. Men with such defenses might be better off taking their cases to a military court rather than entrusting themselves to the program.

In all, the questions about—and the criticisms of—the program doomed it to a hard and uncertain life. The government ordered that ninety-five imprisoned evaders (eligible because they were not also sentenced on other counts) be released while the Clemency Board reviewed their cases. Mr. Ford said that similarly eligible deserters behind bars would be temporarily freed once they had applied to the board. These moves, though demonstrating the government's good faith, did little to inspire men on the outside to step forward.

In the first three days of the program, the Pentagon reported that it received a mere eighty-seven telephone inquiries—and just one letter—from deserters interested in the program. Here and there, a man came in off the streets and presented himself, as did the twenty-two-year-old evader who walked into San Francisco's Federal Building to confess that he had never registered for the draft; he was surprised to learn that the Selective Service System had never heard of him; he admitted that he could have avoided the program altogether by keeping quiet, but added that he was glad to have the chance to clear up his offense. Another evader flew into San Francisco from Canada, tried to get legal help before surrendering himself, found he couldn't afford the fees asked ($500 to $2,500), and flew back to Canada again.

At first, despite the angry reactions of practically all evaders and deserters, it was hoped that the resistance to the program would be temporary. Perhaps the men would cool down in time and see the program as a reasonable one. Perhaps most were not coming forward because they were waiting to see what happened to those of their number who did apply; once they saw that all was well, they would no longer hesitate. Perhaps they were waiting for friends to send them needed information. Perhaps, hoping that there might be a government shift to a full amnesty, they were stalling until the last minute before the January 31, 1975, deadline.

The hopes were many, but they steadily faded as the days and then the weeks passed with hardly a movement homeward. The government had established Indiana's sprawling Camp Atterbury as the center for handling the deserters. It was large enough to accommodate men in large numbers, but on October 15 it was abandoned for lack of business, and the deserter center was transferred to nearby Fort Benjamin Harrison, a much smaller installation.

By November the program's statistics were truly disheartening. Of all the deserters possibly eligible, only 1,481 had applied—and, of these, five hundred were men who were presently serving time. Out of the 120,000 resisters considered eligible to approach the Clemency Board, a scant 560 had applied. And, as for the evaders said to be at large and eligible, just sixty-six had turned themselves in. No more than fifty-seven men had returned from Canada, and only ten from Sweden.

By year's end, it was clear that the resistance was not temporary. On November 29, President Ford tried to break the deadlock by publicly pardoning eighteen men whose names had been submitted to him by the Clemency Board. With newsmen looking on—and with board chairman Goodell and board members Walt and Jordan standing behind him—he granted a full pardon to eight of the men and a conditional clemency to the remaining ten, who were now to complete terms of alternative service ranging from three to twelve months.

The President told the surrounding newsmen that "I could have signed these decisions in a routine way" but that he was making a ceremony of the matter because "I want to use this occasion to underline the commitment of my administration to an even-handed policy of clemency."

But his efforts were in vain. No rush of men followed—only a trickle. Obviously, the resisters had meant what they had said right at the beginning—that the program was useless and an insult to them. Obviously, they saw it as punishment. Obviously, they did not trust the government. Obviously, some of their number had established families and careers for themselves abroad, while others, regardless of their yearnings for home, were committed to stay where they were until they were vindicated with full amnesty.

One young resister living in Canada seemed to sum up the feelings of all his fellows when he remarked: "It would be good to go home, yes. But don't get the idea that I'm just pining to be back. I'll make out here okay. I won't go back to be punished. Only to be cleared, only to hear the U.S. admit it was wrong. Only then. That much I owe myself and everybody else."

January 1975 dawned. Throughout the month the last vestiges of hope for the program faded. There was no late-hour rush to apply. A government campaign of radio and television announcements explaining the program was planned and abandoned. The Clemency Board thought it might write letters to some 8,700 men but said that most of the letters would probably arrive too late to do any good. Government totals of the men who had responded to the program were dismal. The Clemency Board had handled just 890 applicants; so far, some sort of presidential clemency had been granted to sixty-five of that number. The Department of Defense had been approached by 2,627 men, and the Department of Justice by a mere 167.

Hope was reborn—but briefly—in the closing days of January. President Ford, saying that he wanted to give every man the greatest chance possible to apply, extended the program deadline to the end of February, and then to the end of March. The flow of applicants increased significantly, but still did not turn into a last-minute flood. The program closed at midnight, March 31, 1975. The government reported the following figures:

The Presidential Clemency Board had received 18,000 applications to date; it had reviewed several hundred cases and had referred sixty-five to Mr. Ford for presidential action. Of the sixty-five cases sent to Mr. Ford, approximately one-third had been granted outright pardons. Another one-third had been assigned three months of alternative service, and the final one-third had been given longer terms of service, the longest being one year. The board was to continue its review work through 1976.

The Department of Defense had handled 5,253 cases. The Department of Justice had received 603 applications.

In all, 23,856 deserters and evaders had signed up for the program out of the approximate 149,000 men that the government had estimated to be eligible. Charles Goodell, chairman of the Clemency Board, called the program "reasonably successful."

But, for many Americans, the program had been anything but a success. Just less than 20 percent of the men eligible had applied. Still living under a cloud were approximately 125,000 Americans here and abroad. And still with their problem unresolved were all the men whom the program had not embraced—those 450,000 veterans who had been given undesirable or less-than-honorable discharges.

Altogether, a staggering total of at least 575,000 young Americans still remained alienated from the mainstream of their nation's life.

A FINAL NOTE:
A LOOK TO THE FUTURE

The problem of amnesty continues to puzzle Americans everywhere. It has boiled itself down to a single question: What does the future hold for some 575,000 young Americans?

At present, the possibilities are several.

Unconditional Amnesty

The ACLU and all other organizations supporting full amnesty continue to strive for an unconditional amnesty for every man— deserter, evader, and questionably discharged veteran alike—who ran afoul of the military. The determination to press on toward that goal was recently expressed by Arlie Schardt, associate director of the ACLU's Washington, D.C., office. Writing in *Civil Liberties*, the ACLU's monthly news magazine, he called the Ford program incomplete and unfair. "Because no other plan short of unconditional amnesty is either administratively possible . . . or possibly fair, unconditional amnesty is the only solution. . . . Every American determined to bring justice to this tragedy should be writing to his or her Senators and Representatives, insisting on congressional passage of unconditional amnesty as soon as possible."

There seems little hope, however, for unconditional amnesty in the near future unless the President and the Congress are faced with an overwhelming public demand for it. By the very nature of his program President Ford has indicated his unwillingness to consider full amnesty. His is a feeling shared by many congressmen and by many of their constituents. Unconditional amnesty seems no more than a remote possibility until that time—should it ever come—when sympathy for the idea is to be found in the White House, in a preponderance of Congress, and in a strikingly clear majority of the American people.

Presidential Action

Mr. Ford has the freedom to reopen his program at any time so that additional men may take advantage of it. Whether he would ever choose to do so is questionable.

On the one hand, the President is in the position of being able to say that he has done all that he justifiably can for the men and that his offer of help has been rejected—rejected after he had generously extended its deadline on two occasions. On the other hand, pressure from the public and the Congress might induce him to a change of mind. Too, he could decide that, after more time has passed and tempers have further cooled, a reopened program might receive a heartier welcome than was the original case.

Congressional Action

In the wake of the Ford plan, three senators have placed amnesty bills in Congress.

Senators Gaylord Nelson and Jacob Javits have authored a bill calling for the reinstatement of Mr. Ford's program. The bill would extend the program indefinitely and would provide the men with a full chance to take advantage of it. Each man living abroad would be given a thirty-day nonimmigrant pass yearly to return home to visit his family. While here, he could look into the program. Should he not like what he sees, he would be free to return abroad without hindrance. He could then come back the next year for another visit and further consideration of the program.

Senator Nelson is the co-author of yet another amnesty bill. With Senator Philip Hart, he has written a measure awarding full amnesty to all deserters and evaders.

Congress, as of this date, has not acted on the two bills.

The Hatfield Plan

Proposed by Senator Mark Hatfield early in the 1970s, this plan has found approval among people who support conditional amnesty. The senator wrote of it in the book *Amnesty: The Unsettled Question of Vietnam.* He described it as being divided into two parts—one part for evaders, the other for deserters.

When speaking of the evaders, the senator divided them into two categories: (1) those in jail, those awaiting trial, and those who have completed their sentences; and (2) those still at large, whether living here or abroad.

For the men in the first category, he urged a full amnesty, a clearing of their records, a restoration of their full rights as citizens, and the immediate release of those of their number still in jail. They were men, the senator said, who now deserve their freedom because they had honorably faced the consequences of their actions. He set only one restriction: the amnesty would not be extended to any evader who had harmed anyone or destroyed government property.

As for the second category, Senator Hatfield recognized that the evaders who went into hiding or exile had suffered by being cut off from their families, friends, and communities. We should, he wrote, respect the moral commitment behind their action and feel compassion for their suffering. "But," he added, "this does not mean we can blindly endorse their violation of the law."

He advised that a system be developed whereby the evaders could surface or return home to argue that their objection to the war had been truly moral and in good conscience. If a man could prove to the authorities that his conscientious objection had been valid, then he should be granted amnesty and protected against further investigation, arrest, and prosecution. Should he fail to present a convincing case, he should be given a thirty-day period of immunity from arrest so that he could wind up his affairs and leave the country.

During the grace period, he would not be immune from arrest for other violations of the law. After thirty days, he would be liable for prosecution for draft evasion.

Senator Hatfield recommended that "Amnesty Appeal Councils" be established to hear the evaders, one council per circuit of the U.S. Court of Appeals. The cases would come to the councils via the Selective Service System and the Justice Department. The SSS and the Department of Justice would have the power to grant amnesties indirectly, doing so by simply dismissing a case and not referring it to the councils. In all, the system would not overload any council with cases and thus would speed the process of hearing the men.

Each council, the senator advised, should have three members, none of whom "shall have served on state or local draft boards or in the Selective Service System." Each evader, when presenting his case, should not be bound by the current legal requirement for conscientious objection—that the objection be to all war. His case should be judged on the validity of his objection to the Vietnam war only.

When considering the deserters, Senator Hatfield also divided them into two groups—those who had fled under fire and those who had not.

He said flatly that amnesty should not be awarded to the deserters in the first group. Their flight had left the lives of their fellow soldiers in grave peril. The flight had been criminal and should be treated as such.

But, as the senator saw it, the men who had not deserted under fire had not imperiled the lives of others. Their offense was far less serious, and so their cases could be reviewed for amnesty.

He suggested that a six-man board—consisting of three civilians and three military men—be appointed to consider all cases of desertion. It would look into two basic questions in each case: (1) What were the individual's conscientious objections to the war? (2) Did his desertion pose a threat to the lives of the men around him? Depending on the answers, it could then take either of two steps.

First, it could settle the case by granting a man one of several discharges from the service—discharges ranging from the general to the dishonorable. Second, it could refer the case back to the man's branch of service with recommendations as to how he was to be punished. Any deserter wishing to appeal the board's decision could turn to the White House. The President would have the power to grant amnesties to any and all he deemed proper, whether the cases came to him on appeal or not.

"In no case, however," Senator Hatfield cautioned, should amnesties "be granted for acts of violence against persons or property."

As for the board's caseload, the load and the length of time that the board must work could be kept to a minimum by allowing the service branches to award amnesties on their own. The branches would not declare outright amnesties for any of their men, but, in an arrangement like that for the evaders, would simply not refer certain cases to the board, cases that they saw no reason to contest. In any case not sent to the board, the man would be released from the service, given a general discharge, and made to forfeit his pay from the time of his absence.

Senator Hatfield recognized that many Americans felt that the deserters, in putting on a uniform, had made a decision to accept military service and so were obligated to complete that service honorably, regardless of their personal feelings. In effect, they had agreed to a contract and had no right to break it. To that argument, he replied:

"For many of the men who served during the Vietnam war era, the military was the lesser of several evils when compared to jail or self-imposed exile for draft refusal. To refuse amnesty for these men and those who volunteered because they did not come to oppose the war until they actually confronted it, while extending it to those who came to this realization earlier and were articulate enough to establish their position or were able to flee the country, would be to exacerbate existing justice in our land. That simply would not be fair or just to all concerned. . . ."

For his plan for deserters, he had these closing words: "The procedure . . . fully reflects the more complex difficulties encountered by those who deserted. It totally recognizes their abridgment of serious obligations, and the criminal culpability that is entailed. Yet it provides the flexibility necessary if the standard of justice regarding the dictates of conscience are to be extended to all."

These, then, are among the possibilities for the future. But will any of them work? Will any of them satisfy all—or a major segment—of today's American public?

The answer assuredly seems to be "no." Any measure short of unconditional amnesty is bound to outrage all who support the views of the ACLU and the remaining deserters and evaders. All feel that the civil rights of countless Americans were violated during the Vietnam years. Nothing less than full and unconditional amnesty is acceptable. Without it, justice will not have been done and national honor will not have been restored.

Conversely, unconditional amnesty is bound to outrage all those who favor no-amnesty. They continue to see the desertions and evasions as a threat to the country's legal and social fabric. In their eyes, unconditional amnesty will intensify that threat for the future. Conditional amnesty—a "slap on the hand" when firm measures are needed—will constitute a similar threat.

And so the puzzle remains. The future is clouded. Will time take care of the matter, enabling conflicting groups at last to arrive at some compromise solution? Or will public opinion eventually so shift to unconditional amnesty that it can be granted without widespread acrimony? Or will today's President or Congress—or some future President or Congress—decide on a final action regardless of public opinion? Or will some as-yet-undreamed-of solution finally mark the end of the whole question?

No one knows.

Only one thing can be said for certain. No matter what the answer proves to be, the puzzle must be solved.

A SELECTED READING LIST

Those interested in studying further the amnesty question and the Vietnam debate will find the following books to be of particular help:

Affluent Revolutionaries: A Portrait of the New Left, Stephen Goode; New York: Franklin Watts, Inc., 1974.

Amnesty: The Unsettled Question of Vietnam, Arlie Schardt, William A. Rusher, and Mark O. Hatfield; Lawrence, Massachusetts: Sun River Press and Two Continents Publishing Group, 1973.

Anatomy of Error, Henry Brandon; Boston: Gambit, Inc., 1969.

How the U.S. Got Involved in Vietnam, Robert Scheer; Santa Barbara, California: Center for the Study of Democratic Institutions and the Fund for the Republic, Inc., 1965.

The New Exiles, Roger Neville Williams; New York: Liveright Publishers, 1971.

They Can't Go Home Again: The Story of America's Political Refugees, Richard L. Killmer, Robert S. Lecky, and Debrah S. Wiley; Philadelphia: Pilgrim Press, 1971.

Tigers in the Rice, Walter J. Sheldon; New York: Crowell-Collier Press, 1969.

Vietnam: Crisis of Conscience, Robert McAfee Brown, Abraham J. Heschel, and Michael Novak; New York: Association Press, Behrman House, and Herder and Herder, 1967.

Waiting Out a War, Lucinda Franks; New York: Coward, McCann & Geoghegan, Inc., 1974.

INDEX